Steve Schmi

Fly Fishing Utah

A Quick, Clear Understanding of Where to Fly Fish in Utah

NO NONSENSE

FLY FISHING GUIDEBOOKS

Author
Steve Schmidt

Maps, Illustrations, and Production
Pete Chadwell, *Dynamic Arts*
Gary D. Smith, *Performance Design*

Front Cover Photo
Alan O'Connor

Back Cover Photo
Alan O'Connor

Editors
Jim Yuskavitch and David Banks

Published By
No Nonsense Fly Fishing Guidebooks
P.O. Box 91858
Tucson AZ 85752-1858

Printed in USA

Disclaimer
While this guide will greatly help fly fishers, it is not a substitute for caution, good judgment, and the services of a qualified fly fishing guide or outfitter.

©2004 Steve Schmidt

ISBN 10: 0-9637256-8-8
ISBN 13: 978-0-9637256-8-4
ISBN 13: 978-1-61881-235-3 (ebook)

No Nonsense Fly Fishing Guidebooks believes that in addition to local information and gear, fly fishers need clean water and healthy fish. The publisher encourages preservation, improvement, conservation, enjoyment, and understanding of our waters and their inhabitants. A good way to do this is to support organizations dedicated to these ideas.

Where No Nonsense Guides Come From

No Nonsense guidebooks give you a quick, clear, understanding of the essential information needed to fly fish a region's most outstanding waters. The authors are highly experienced and qualified local fly fishers. Maps are tidy versions of the author's sketches.

These guides are produced by the fly fishers, their friends, and spouses of fly fishers, at No Nonsense Fly Fishing Guidebooks.

All who produce No Nonsense guides believe in providing top quality products at a reasonable price. We also believe all information should be verified. We never hesitate to go out, fly rod in hand, to verify the facts and figures that appear in the pages of these guides. The staff is committed to this research. It's dirty work, but we're glad to do it for you.

Contents

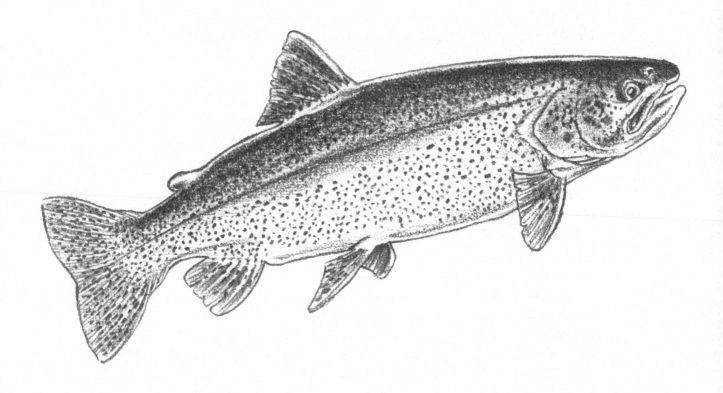

Rainbow Trout

Dedication

Today fly fishing plays a large role in my life.
Without the support and involvement
of my family, however, it would have little significance.
I dedicate this work to family and friends.

To my mom and dad, who gave me great opportunities,
in life with their constant support and guidance.

To my best friends:
Ann, my wife, and Mike and Maggie, my kids,
who make life worthwhile.

To Emmett Heath,
my fly fishing mentor and friend.

I owe them all.

Acknowledgments

Many people were involved in putting these pages together, and their efforts helped make this book a pleasant endeavor as well as a more complete guide.

First of all, I'd like to thank David Banks, whose patience, energy, perseverance, and vision gave me a much greater appreciation for those involved in writing and publishing books. Steve Cook supplied editing expertise in addition to a great deal of information about many of these fisheries. Thank you, Steve; your guidance and knowledge of Utah waters were very instrumental in many aspects of this publication. I'm fortunate to work with a great staff, including Andy Fitzhugh, Greg Pearson, and Jon Jackson. Their individual and combined knowledge and expertise also contributed significantly to the completion of this project. Kevin Moser, one of our guides with whom I had never fished until I asked him to show me his favorite waters, opened my eyes to the great fishing on the South Fork of the Odgen. Bill Marsden's love of small streams and the Uinta Mountains helped simplify a vast wilderness area. Although some of my early fly fishing experiences took place around Logan, Darren Gardner put the finishing touches on this area's great waters. Jim "Road Kill" Keyser lived in and fished southern Utah for most of his adult life, and his help with the Antimony Creek and Pine Lake sections was invaluable. Bud Murray and Bill Young are a couple of complete anglers whose combined knowledge and passion for fly fishing is a rare thing these days. John Campbell enthusiastically provided information about the spectacular area of the Boulder Mountains, and I'm sure his clients get the same unselfish effort when they use his services in this beautiful area. Finally, I'd like to thank my family for being understanding about all the time I took away from them to pursue this endeavor.

This book has certainly been a group effort, and I greatly appreciate the contributions of everyone who lent support. I owe a great deal of thanks to all of them.

Foreword

My goal in writing this No Nonsense Guide to Fly Fishing Utah was to give readers the best, most accurate information available. Because my personal fly fishing experiences cannot cover a state the size of Utah, I felt it was important to use as many different sources as possible to create a viable destination resource. Consequently, much of what is written here draws on the expertise of some of the most competent fly anglers found in Utah to supplement my own. Without their assistance and cooperation, this book would not be as complete or thorough.

When reading this guidebook, please keep in mind that it is just that, a guide. As even a novice fly angler realizes, weather, water flows, angling pressure, and other conditions that affect fishing are in a constant state of flux. Simply put, you get what you get when you get there.

The most anglers can do to enhance their day or week of fishing is to prepare as much as possible for the wide variety of conditions they might encounter at their chosen fishing destination. The value of this guide lies in its ability to assist you with your general preparations. It will help you select the right equipment, the best flies, and the most productive water for the time of year you want to fish. To make the most out of your outing, however, I still highly recommend that you either call or stop by a local fly shop for the most current conditions. This combination of general preparation and current information will go a long way toward ensuring a successful fly fishing experience.

The waters described in this guidebook offer Utah's best fishing. Rating them, however, was the most difficult aspect of this whole project. Fly fishing is a very personal and subjective sport, and consequently, everyone's expectations are different. For instance, how do scenery and solitude stack up against number of hookups when rating a fishery? In these pages, I have tried to balance the quality versus quantity issue, but each rating is still colored by my own personal preferences. Again, this is a general guide, and any additional information you can gather can only help in your selection of a fishery that will meet your expectations.

Finally, but most important given the still-growing interest in fly fishing, one of my concerns about guidebooks such as this *Fly Fishing Utah* is the impact the information will have on my state's wonderfully diverse but fragile angling resources. When you visit Utah, you certainly owe it to yourself to sample some of the West's best fly waters, but it is my sincere hope that this guide will not only help you get the most out of your fishing, but also leave you with an appreciation for the beauty and uniqueness of Utah's lakes and streams and the fish that inhabit them. Please treat these resources with respect and care, so that others may share the same quality of experience in the future.

Enjoy the book, and I hope to see you on the stream.

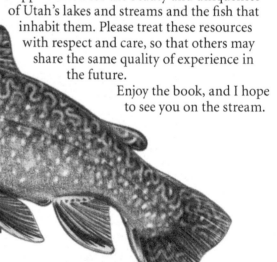

PETE
CHADWELL
2000

Utah Vicinity Map

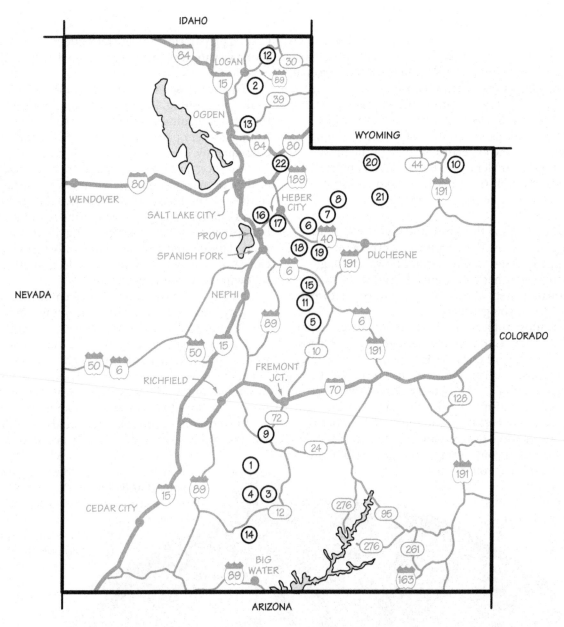

Profiled Streams, Lakes, and Reservoirs

1. Antimony Creek
2. Blacksmith Fork
3. Boulder Mountain, East Side
4. Boulder Mountain, West Side
5. Cottonwood Creek
6. Currant Creek
7. Duchesne River, North Fork
8. Duchesne River, West Fork
9. Fremont River
10. Green River
11. Huntington Creek
12. Logan River
13. Ogden River, South Fork
14. Pine Lake
15. Price River
16. Provo River, Lower
17. Provo River, Middle
18. Strawberry Reservoir
19. Strawberry River
20. Uinta Mountains, North Slope
21. Uinta Mountains, South Slope
22. Weber River

Conditions by Month
Utah Fly Fishing

FEATURED WATERS

(1) REFERS TO NUMBERS ON VICINITY MAP

Legend: ■ BEST ▨ GOOD ▢ FAIR □ NOT FISHABLE

Featured Waters	Jan	Feb	Mar	Apr	May	Jun	Jul	Aug	Sep	Oct	Nov	Dec
(1) Antimony Creek			Fair	Fair	Good	Best	Good	Good	Best	Fair		
(2) Blacksmith Fork	Fair	Fair	Fair	Good	Best	Best	Good	Good	Good	Fair	Fair	
(3)(4) Boulder Mountain					Good	Good	Good	Good	Good	Good		
(5) Cottonwood Creek	Fair	Fair	Fair	Best	Fair			Best	Best	Best	Fair	
(6) Currant Creek	Fair	Fair	Fair				Best	Best	Best	Good		Fair
(7) Duchesne River, North Fork	Fair	Fair	Fair	Good	Good		Best	Best	Best	Good	Fair	
(8) Duchesne River, West Fork	Fair	Fair	Fair		Good	Good	Best	Best	Best	Good	Fair	
(9) Fremont River	Fair	Fair	Good	Good			Best	Best	Best	Good	Fair	
(10) Green River	Fair	Good	Good	Best		Best	Best	Best	Best	Good	Good	Fair
(11) Huntington Creek	Fair	Good	Good	Best		Best	Best	Best	Good	Fair	Best	
(12) Logan River	Fair	Fair	Fair	Good			Best	Best	Best	Good	Fair	
(13) Ogden River, South Fork	Fair	Fair	Fair	Good		Best	Best	Best	Best	Good	Fair	
(14) Pine Lake					Fair	Good	Good	Good	Good			
(15) Price River	Fair	Fair	Fair	Good	Good			Good	Best	Best	Fair	
(16) Provo River, Lower	Fair	Good	Good	Best	Best			Best	Best	Best	Good	Fair
(17) Provo River, Middle	Fair	Good	Fair	Best			Best	Best	Best	Good	Fair	
(18) Strawberry Reservoir					Fair		Best	Best	Best	Good		
(19) Strawberry River	Fair	Fair	Fair	Good			Best	Best	Best	Good	Fair	
(20) Uinta Mountains, North Slope						Best	Best	Best	Good			
(21) Uinta Mountains, South Slope						Best	Best	Best	Good			
(22) Weber River	Fair	Fair	Fair	Good		Best	Best	Best	Best	Best	Good	Fair

The Utah No Nonsense Fly-O-Matic
A Quick-Start Guide for Fly Fishing Utah

Hatches and Water Conditions

As in other western states, in Utah hatches and water conditions constantly change. If you are new to the area, are just getting started, or have not fished in a while, you would be well advised to check out the most up-to-date hatch and water information at a good local fly shop. Regardless of your ability, this knowledge will help make your day a success. Most fly shops can be contacted by phone or over the Internet, but best of all is to visit in person. They are happy to answer any questions you might have as you prepare for your trip or outing.

Weather

Utah's weather is no less diverse than its landscape; give it five minutes, and it will usually change. Knowing that proper clothing and gear can be invaluable, the smart angler is prepared for all kinds of weather regardless of the time of year. At higher elevations especially, changes in the weather can be severe and drastic, with snow being a possibility twelve months out of the year. If you plan to venture far from your car, play it safe and pack extra clothing and a good set of rain gear to ensure that you will be prepared for whatever Mother Nature decides to do.

In addition to proper clothing, having an alternative fishing plan may also save the day if inclement weather vetoes your first choice. Many of Utah's rivers and streams muddy up after an outbreak of heavy, isolated showers, but there is usually other quality water nearby. Given the fact that less-than-optimal weather conditions often coincide with some of the year's best fishing, a little rain or even snow should not deter the well-prepared angler.

Game Fish

As in most of the West, fly fishing in Utah usually means fishing for trout. However, the state boasts other species worth the effort of a well-presented fly. The recent introduction of smallmouth bass into Jordanelle Reservoir has captured the attention of local fly rodders, and Pelican Lake, now making a comeback after years of drought, should regain its reputation for producing very large bluegill. In the southern reaches of the state, Lake Powell, long regarded as a boater's paradise, has excellent populations of striped and largemouth bass that, at the right time of year, provide excellent fly fishing opportunities. In addition, carp, although shunned by serious anglers in the past, is gaining well-deserved recognition as a formidable foe in the fly rod community. The flats of Willard Bay Reservoir and Bear Lake are excellent areas to pursue this under-appreciated game fish.

Catch and Release

Given the popularity of fly fishing and the limited resources available, catch and release should be practiced by everyone. Practicing catch and release, regardless of the regulations, helps to ensure the future of quality fishing for yourself as well as your fellow anglers. If you are not familiar with catch and release, here are a few tips to help you return your fish to the water unharmed.

Use barbless hooks. Since they are much easier to remove, you may not even need to touch the fish you are about to release. These hooks also do less harm if you hook yourself or another angler and save wear-and-tear on the fly itself.

Use a net with a soft bag. Landing fish is much easier, and a soft net bag will not harm or mark a fish. If you do not have a net, remain in the water and "land" the fish in slow currents or eddies. Never drag a fish you plan to release out of the water.

If a fish takes the hook deep, cut the line, even if you are fishing barbless. The hook will quickly rust out, and a healthy fish is far more valuable than a single fly.

Use hemostats or one of the new hook-extraction tools to aid in the removal of the hook.

Always wet your hands before handling any fish. Handle it as little as possible, and never squeeze a fish. If you want to take a picture of your prize catch, keep the fish in the water until you are ready to take the shot. Lift the fish, quickly take the photo, and gently place the fish back in the water.

Hold the fish gently, facing it into the current until it is ready to swim away. If there is no current, gently move the fish back and forth to aid water circulation through its gills.

Hazards and Safety

Do not take lightly the safety issues presented by rivers and still waters. Paying attention to these few tips will help you safely enjoy your fly fishing adventure.

A wading belt is a necessity these days, especially now that lightweight breathable waders are so popular. Waders can easily fill with water if you fall in water, turning a simple misstep into a life-threatening situation. Regardless of what type of waders you are wearing, a snugly cinched-up wading belt eliminates most of this danger.

Although the majority of Utah's rivers and streams are not very large by western standards, these waters can be extremely dangerous and difficult to wade during runoff season. Studded boots and a staff are indispensable in high- or fast-water situations, as well as in the morning and evening when the river bottom is difficult to see.

No matter where or when you fish in the inter-mountain West, hypothermia is always a threat. Ironically, most anglers fall victim to hypothermia during the summer when days that start out dry and warm suddenly turn dark, windy, and wet. The best way to avoid hypothermia is always to be prepared for a variety of weather conditions. Extra clothes, matches in a waterproof container, a few high-energy snacks, and good rain gear may be the most important extra weight you will ever pack on a fishing excursion.

Given the possibility of dehydration posed by Utah's mostly arid climate, also carry a good water filtration bottle as part of your equipment. As inviting as all that water swirling around your knees may look, do not drink it unfiltered. It might taste cool and sweet at the time, but even a mild case of giardia will make you regret your decision. New, lightweight filtration bottles are inexpensive and

effective, allowing you to keep your load light and to drink freely out of most of the waters you fish.

Fly fishing is largely about peace and quiet, and many anglers prefer to spend their fishing time alone. These days, finding a little solitude often means trekking farther than ever off the beaten path. Before you set out on such an excursion, make sure you tell a reliable person where you are going and when you plan to be back. Given the rugged terrain surrounding many of our great waters, this precaution could possibly save your life.

Graphite rods turn anglers into human lightning rods. Whenever lightning is near, find a low spot in the nearby terrain and lay your rod down until the storm passes. Storms are a particular danger on still waters where, in addition to the threat of lightning, high winds that can capsize a small fishing pram or exhaust even the strongest float tuber often accompany sudden summer storms. Caught in such a situation, your best bet is to stop fishing, break your rod down, and quickly make for the nearest shore, even if that means a long walk around the lake to get back to your car.

Many anglers are introducing their kids to the sport of fly fishing. Remember, however, that your children have neither your size nor experience. Water that you may take for granted might pose a hazardous wading situation for a child inexperienced in judging the depth of a stream or unprepared for

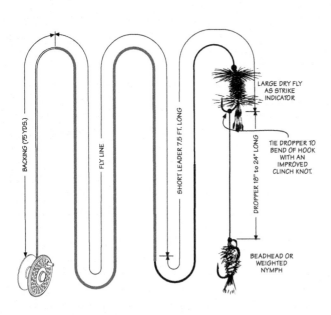

Using a large dry fly as a strike indicator can be very effective in Utah. Use the dry fly as you would any strike indicator, except that it will hook a fish that rolls on it! Tie the dropper directly to the bend of the hook using an improved clinch knot.

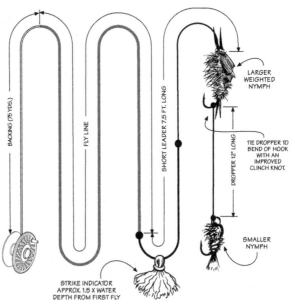

Another popular two-fly rig for fly fishing in Utah uses a typical strike indicator placed on the butt section of the leader roughly 1½ times the water depth from the first fly. Use a large weighted nymph as the first fly, then add a dropper and use a smaller nymph as a trailer.

how powerful currents can be. For their safety and your own peace of mind, always position yourself just a little downstream from the children you are fishing with. If they fall or slip, you will be in a prefect position to help them.

Small Streams

One highlight of fly fishing Utah is its numerous small streams, waters that most fly rodders have paid little attention to in the past. Today, however, there are many short fly rods on the market designed to function in cramped quarters, cast shorter distances, and handle smaller fish. These advances in small rod design, along with significant improvements in reels and lines, will make a big difference in the experience you have on small streams.

Because many anglers are fixated on big fish, small streams experience little fishing pressure on most days. As a result, the fish in these waters are generally opportunistic in their fly selection, but just because they are not picky does not mean they are not also easily spooked. In fact, you will find that these are some of the most skittish fish around. Since they have not become accustomed to a parade of anglers walking past them, most small-stream fish will dart for cover at the first unnatural sight or sound. Approach these small streams with caution, wade carefully, and watch where your shadow falls for the most success.

Although the trout found in most small waters are not selective, it still pays to have a good selection of flies. Many streams have a good diversity of aquatic insects that produce excellent hatches. For example, several of the state's small streams have the famous green drake hatch, but if you do not have a #10 Mayfly Dun in your box, you are in for a frustrating day. Equip yourself with a good selection of Caddis and Mayfly adults, as well as nymphs, streamers, and leeches, and you will be well prepared for any situation on Utah's smaller streams.

High-Elevation Lakes and Streams

The spectacular Boulder and Uinta mountains are home to literally hundreds of Utah's pristine and spectacular fly fishing resources. Although many are just off the beaten path, others require serious planning and a fair amount of effort to reach. If you would like to explore the waters of either of these ranges, remember that the maps provided in this guide lack detail and are not to scale. These maps by no means accurately reflect distances, elevation changes, difficulty of access, or hiking time necessary to reach some of the highlighted waters. For example, reaching Red Castle Lake (shown on the Uinta North map) requires a long, strenuous hike into a wilderness surrounded by peaks exceeding 12,000 feet in elevation. A trip into this area is by no means a simple day hike, and before heading out, you need to do your homework. Consult someone who has been to your destination before, secure a good set of topographic maps, and make sure that you have the necessary hiking and camping equipment to visit and fish these beautiful areas.

Runoff Season

When Utah's runoff season begins, the duration and overall impact on our fishing resources are dependent on the weather. During a warm year, runoff can start as early as April; or it can end as late as the end of June, if there is a cold, wet spring. May is typically when the state's rivers and streams are swollen with snowmelt, but because temperatures run warmer in the central and southern portions of the state, runoff usually begins and ends two weeks earlier there than in the northern regions. The good news is that the state has many tailwater fisheries unaffected by runoff. If you planning to visit Utah between late April and early June, rest assured that you will be able to find a few quality waters that will provide a memorable fly fishing experience.

Special Techniques

Utah's lakes and streams are home to a wide variety of aquatic and terrestrial insects that produce some amazing hatches. To take advantage of the diversity and size of these hatching insects, anglers traditionally fish two-fly, deep nymphing systems that are time consuming to rig and difficult to cast. On some of our smaller waters, these systems are also inappropriate. The two-fly rigs on page 11 are quick to set up and easy to cast while still allowing you effectively to address a variety of hatches and fishing situations.

A favorite technique is to fish a subsurface emerger or nymph pattern under a floating adult pattern. Attached to the dry, the subsurface pattern is fished in or just under the surface film. Because the nymph or emerger is difficult to see, especially under low light conditions, the dry fly in this technique acts as a strike indicator. This floating pattern should closely resemble the adult insect you are trying to match, but most of all, it should be easy to locate on the water. The fishes' ability to see this fly is crucial to the success of this system, so if need be, do not hesitate to use a dry fly a size larger than the actual insect. The dropper nymph or emerger pattern should be attached to the bend of the dry fly's hook with an appropriate-sized tippet that extends no farther than 18 inches. This very effective system assembles easily and casts effortlessly.

Another popular two-fly rig combines a large stonefly or terrestrial pattern with a beadhead nymph.

In April, the first stoneflies begin to emerge, and after runoff subsides in June, the larger golden stones and salmonflies also appear. This is also the time when Utah's excellent populations of hoppers, large ants, and cicadas become important to fly anglers. The size and buoyancy of these large insects make them excellent lead flies in a two-fly system that includes larger or heavier subsurface patterns. Both the dry and nymph patterns in this system should be sizes #4 to #8. If there is sufficient room, attach the appropriate-sized tippet through the eye of the lead fly. This arrangement positions the heavy nymph directly under the high-floating dry. Because the dropper pattern in this system is large and heavy, your tippet can range from 18 to 36 inches long, allowing you to fish deeper water. Again, this is a very quick and easy dropper system to assemble and fish.

Rods, Reels, and Lines

This guide recommends rods, reels, and lines for every profiled water. However, an 8½- to 9-foot fly rod with a 5 weight line will address almost any fishing situation you will encounter in Utah. A fly reel with enough drag to prevent backlash when line is pulled off will also make your day on the stream or lake more enjoyable. A simple, single-action, click-pawl or disc reel with an adjustable drag will more than suffice. For most of Utah's fly fishing, a floating line is your best option. However, if you plan to spend the majority of your time on reservoirs or lakes, a type-2 full-sink line or type-4 sink tip will allow you to fly fish these waters more effectively.

Private Property

Unlike in other western states, in Utah there is no access through private property below the high-water mark. If a stream or river passes through their property, landowners own the stream bottom. Because many anglers have misunderstood or disregarded this law in the past, it is now much more difficult to gain permission to fish from landowners who were once amenable to granting access. Please respect property owners' rights. Some of Utah's fishable waters also flow through the state's several Indian reservations. Remember that waters that pass through these lands are governed by tribal laws and regulations and require special permits to fish. For sources of information regarding access, licensing, and regulations that apply to Utah fishing, please refer to the numbers and addresses listed in the back of this book.

Float Tubes, Kick Boats, Rafts, etc.

In Utah, anything a person can use as a means of transportation on water, including float tubes, kick boats, rafts, etc., falls under the definition of a boat.

On moving water, every person in a boat, from inner tubes to drift boats, must wear a Coast Guard approved personal flotation device (PFD). On still waters, you must carry at least one approved PFD for every person in the boat. For more specifics on PFD requirements and considerations, consult a current Utah Fishing Proclamation. Authorities do not take boating safety lightly here in Utah, and if you are cited, fines are not cheap.

Steve Schmidt. Photo by Alan O'Connor.

Common Game Fish in Utah

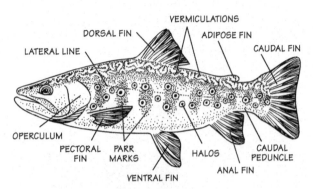

Typical salmon, trout, or char.
Most hatchery fish have a clipped adipose fin.

GRAYLING
This member of the whitefish family is silvery gray with black spots. The very large dorsal fin is spotted with blue and edged with pink. Ventral fins are striped with purple.

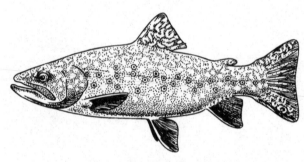

BROOK TROUT
"Brookies" are in the char family (Dolly, bull trout, lake trout, etc.). Back is black, blue-gray, or green with mottled, light-colored markings. Sides have red spots with blue rings. Tail is square. Lower fins are red, striped with black and white. Prefers colder water.

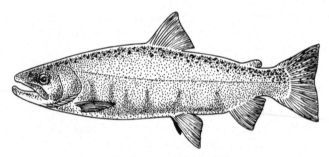

KOKANEE SALMON
The back is green-blue with speckles. The head is green. Sides and belly are silver. During fall spawning, color turns to dark red. Skin is leathery. Male snout hooks and back humps while the female body shape stays like a trout.

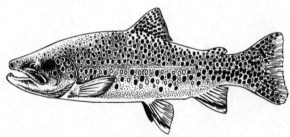

BROWN TROUT
The brown back has big black spots.
The tail is square, and the sides have black and red spots with light blue rings. It's hard to catch and easily spooked.

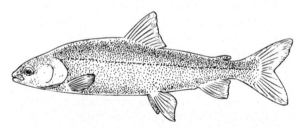

MOUNTAIN WHITEFISH
Color is light brown or bronze to whitish, tail is split. Mouth is smaller than a trout's and doesn't extend back past the eye.

CUTTHROAT TROUT
Dark green back, flanks are golden to pink in color with black spots that increase in number towards the tail. The red jaw is the most telling marking.

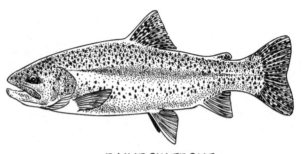

RAINBOW TROUT
The most abundant wild and hatchery fish. It has an olive-bluish back with small black spots. Each side has a light red or pink band. Lake 'bows are often all silver.

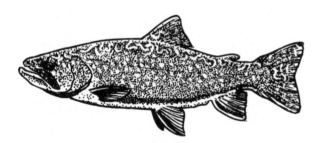

SPLAKE
A fertile hybrid of brook trout and lake trout, its name comes from combining "speckled trout," a common name for brook trout, with "lake." Appearance is very similar to brook trout, but without the bright red spots and blue halos.
Tail is slightly forked.

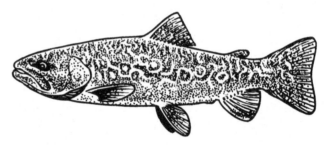

TIGER TROUT
This rare hybrid between brown and brook trout is distinguished by dark brown vermiculations on the sides against a pale orange or yellowish base. Fins are orange. Another very similar hybrid is the Brake, a cross between a male brown and a female lake trout.

Illustrations by Pete Chadwell. For fine art and fish renderings, contact www.dynamicarts.biz.

Utah Hatch Chart

INSECTS ▨ BEST HATCH ACTIVITY	JANUARY	FEBRUARY	MARCH	APRIL	MAY	JUNE	JULY	AUGUST	SEPTEMBER	OCTOBER	NOVEMBER	DECEMBER
Ants						▨	▨	▨	▨			
Beetles						▨	▨	▨				
Blue-Winged Olives		▨	▨	▨				▨	▨	▨	▨	
Caddis						▨	▨	▨	▨			
Callibaetis					▨	▨	▨					
Cicadas					▨	▨	▨					
Golden Stoneflies						▨	▨					
Green Drakes					▨	▨	▨					
Hoppers							▨	▨	▨			
Little Salmonflies				▨	▨							
Little Yellow Sallies						▨	▨					
Mahogany Duns									▨	▨		
Midges	▨	▨	▨	▨	▨	▨	▨	▨	▨	▨	▨	
Pale Morning Duns						▨	▨	▨				
Salmonflies						▨	▨					
Tricos							▨	▨	▨			

The Best Flies to Use in Utah

ARTICULATED LEECH

BEADHEAD HARE'S EAR

BEADHEAD PEACOCK STONE

BEADHEAD PHEASANT TAIL

BEADHEAD PRINCE

BURKE'S DAMSEL

CHAMOIS CADDIS

CLOUSER MINNOW

DAMSEL NYMPH

DAVE'S HOPPER

DIVING CADDIS

DOUBLE MIDGE

ELK HAIR CADDIS

HI-VIS GRIFFITH'S GNAT

HUMPY

KAUFMAN'S STONE

LAWSON'S EMERGING CADDIS

MARK'S CICADA

MUDDLER MINNOW

PARACHUTE ADAMS

PMD CRIPPLE

ROYAL WULFF

SCHROEDER'S PARA-HOPPER

SHIMAZAKI ANT

SOFT HACKLE MIDGE

SOWBUG

SPARKLE DUN

STIMULATOR

WOOLLY BUGGER

ZONKER

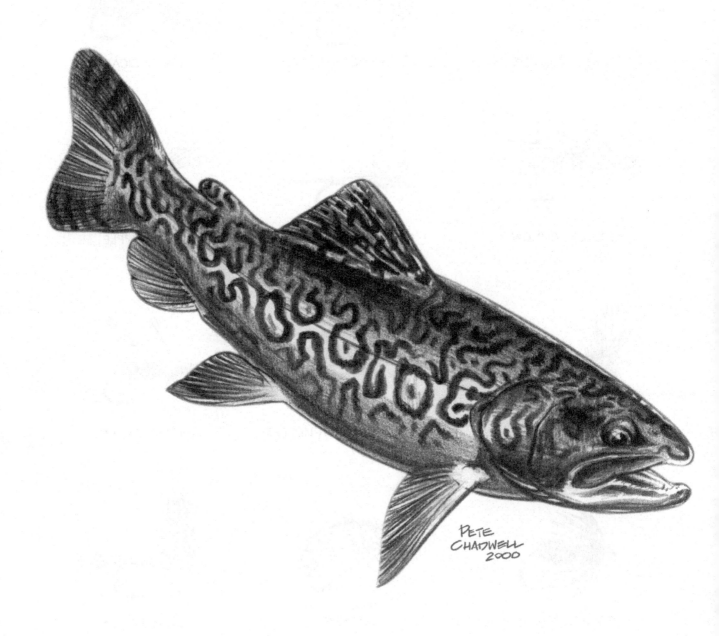

Utah's Tiger Trout

Top Utah Fly Fishing Waters

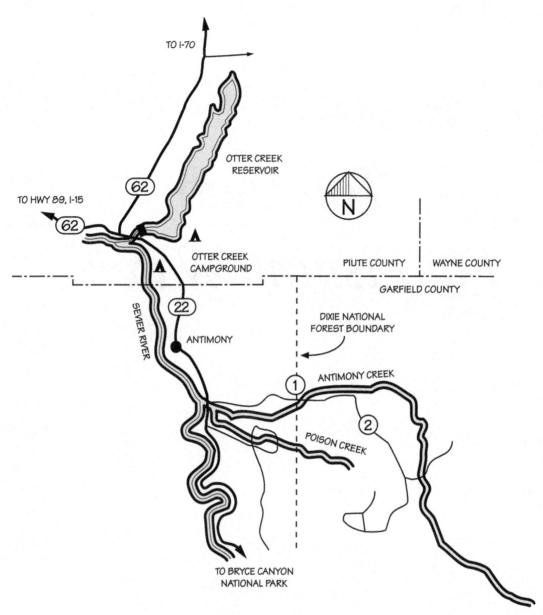

① From this point downstream is mostly private property and runs dry at times.
② Road gets rough—4WD necessary, especially in wet weather.

Note: There are no developed campgrounds along the creek. However, there are areas where camping is permitted.

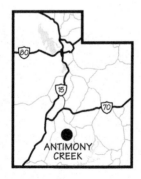

ANTIMONY CREEK

NOT TO SCALE

Antimony Creek

As you travel south, Utah's spectacular granite peaks, glaciated valleys, and subalpine meadows give way to equally breathtaking red rock. Here, due to the region's arid climate, recreational and fishing considerations must often give way to irrigation demands on available water. Nevertheless, the determined angler can still discover some very productive trout water, as evidenced by Antimony Creek.

Tumbling cold and clear out of the high elevations of the Dixie National Forest, Antimony Creek is typical of Utah's many small streams. Shaded by cottonwoods and dense willows and barely 30 feet across at the most, this little jewel of a freestone stream holds trout that average 10 to 12 inches with the occasional trophy of 16 inches. For the angler who enjoys fishing a small rod, this stream and its trout more than fit the bill.

Antimony Creek's predominant insects are caddisflies with terrestrials providing a secondary yet important source of food. If you enjoy fishing dries, the creek's trout are more than a little fond of them. Although not especially particular about pattern shape, these wild fish can be fussy about size. Flies, specifically Caddis patterns, should run #16–18 to be most effective.

There's a fairly good dirt road leading to Antimony Creek; however, due to inconsistent flows, don't bother fishing the stream just above its confluence with Poison Creek and the Sevier River just after it exits the USFS boundary line. After several miles, the road gives way to a trail up a narrow sandstone canyon that provides shelter for wild rainbows and browns, just waiting for a meal in this beautiful little creek's cool riffles and deep, clear pools. Could there be a more pleasant way to spend the day?

Types of Fish
Rainbow and brown trout.

Known Hatches
Little yellow sallies, ants, beetles, blue-winged olives, and caddisflies.

Equipment to Use
Rods: 0–5 weight, 7–9'.
Reels: Click or disc standard trout reel.
Lines: Weight forward or double-taper floating lines.
Leaders: 4X to 7X, 7–9'.
Waders: Hip waders or breathable lightweights during the colder months. Wet-wading during the summer months is quite pleasant.

Flies to Use
Dry Patterns: Tan Elk Hair Caddis #16–18; Goddard Caddis #16; Peacock Caddis #16–18; Black or Cinnamon Fur Ant #18; Shimazaki Ant (Black or Cinnamon) #16; Parachute Adams #18; Royal Wulff #16–18; Red or Yellow Humpy #16; Olive and Yellow Stimulators #16.
Nymphs: Pheasant Tail #18; Hare's Ear #16–18; Chamois Caddis #16; Peeking Caddis #16–18; Prince #16. Beadhead versions of all patterns will work nicely fished alone or as a dropper below a dry fly.
Streamers: In the fall, streamers can be effective, but given the size of the water, they should be sparse and small: Muddler Minnow; Light Spruce Fly; Olive, Blood, and Black Leech, all #6–8.

When to Fish
Because Antimony Creek is located in the southern part of the state, runoff ends relatively early. The best time to fish is from June through July.

Seasons & Limits
Year-round. General fishing regulations apply; check current regulations.

Accommodations & Services
Camping is your best option. There are facilities at Otter Creek State Park and other campgrounds around the reservoir.

Nearby Fly Fishing
Sevier River and Otter Creek Reservoir offer some fly fishing opportunities, but favorable conditions are not consistent. Also try Pine Lake.

Rating
Compared to other small streams in the area, Antimony Creek is a 7. It offers excellent fly fishing for wild rainbow and brown trout, but these fish are smaller than those found in other similar waters.

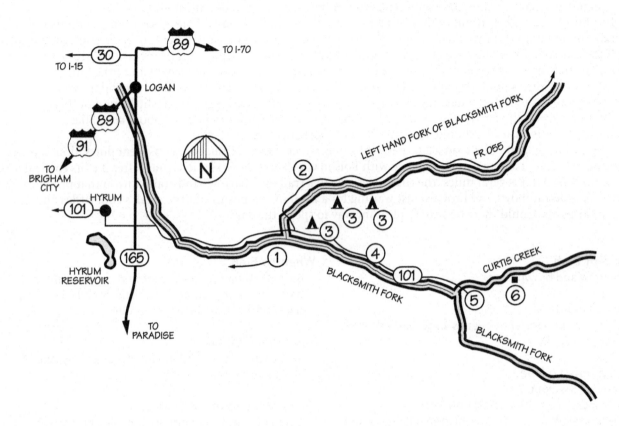

1. Predominantly pocket water—caddisflies and stoneflies abundant.
2. Dirt road.
3. Maintained campgrounds with minimal facilities.
4. Best dry fly water.
5. Limited access due to private property.
6. The Hardware Ranch—home to thousands of elk that winter here.

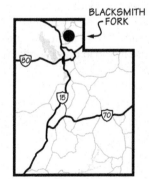

BLACKSMITH FORK

NOT TO SCALE

Blacksmith Fork

The Cache Valley has more fly shops per capita than anywhere else in Utah. This is not necessarily surprising given the number of quality fishing waters within a short distance of this scenic rural area—waters like Blacksmith Fork, which over the years has been one of the more productive trout streams in the state.

A medium-sized piece of water by western standards, Blacksmith Fork is nevertheless a diverse and challenging fishery. From a small, subalpine stream gaining volume as it cascades through the canyon to the quality freestone water of the lower river, it offers a variety of options for the fly fisher. There is even a small section with spring creek-like conditions above a small hydroelectric dam about halfway downstream.

Among Blacksmith Fork's plentiful hatches, the dominant insect is the caddisfly. Midsummer heat brings on late-evening caddis hatches that typically produce some of the river's best fly fishing. These hatches occur quickly, however, often during the last hours of daylight. At such times, the difficult part of the equation is not selecting a fly—the trout are seldom selective—but tying it on and finding it once it's on the water. These circumstances have left more than one fly fisher out in the dark, so to speak. Make sure you take a light.

Blacksmith Fork's richly oxygenated lower stretches are also home to the largest and most famous fly in trout fishing, *Pteronarcys californica*. As any angler who has fished more than a few years knows, these insects, more commonly known as salmonflies, always bring fish to the surface, providing a real opportunity to catch a trophy trout on a dry fly.

Types of Fish
Wild brown and cutthroat trout as well as stocked rainbows.

Known Hatches
Salmonflies, golden stoneflies, little yellow sallies, pale morning duns, blue-winged olives, caddisflies, hoppers, ants, beetles, and cicadas.

Equipment to Use
Rods: 4–6 weight, 8–9'.
Reels: Standard click or disc trout reel.
Lines: Weight forward or double-taper floating and occasionally a sinking or sink tip line for streamers.
Leaders: 4X to 5X, 7–12'.
Wading: Lightweight or neoprene chest-high waders and felt-soled boots.

Flies to Use
Dry Patterns: Improved Salmon Fly #4; Lawson's Salmon Fly #4–6; Yellow Stimulators #8 or #14; AK's Quill Body PMD #16; PMD Sparkle Dun #16; PMD Cripple #16; Rusty Spinner #16; BWO Sparkle Dun #18; BWO Cripple #16; Cicada #10; Parachute Hopper #6–10; Cinnamon Shimazaki Ant #16; Spent Partridge Caddis #14–18; Lawson's Emerging Caddis tan; Elk Hair Caddis; Royal Wulff #14–20.
Nymphs: Kaufman's Stone #4–6; Peacock Stone #4–8; Prince #12; Red Fox Squirrel Hair #8–14; Z–Wing Caddis; Peeking Caddis; Tan Diving Caddis #14; Pheasant Tail #16–20; Hare's Ear #16–18; and WD-40 #18–20; all with or without a Beadhead.

Streamers: Muddler Minnow #4–10; Articulated Leech; Yellow Marabou Muddler; Olive Spruce Fly #4; Black, Peacock, or Olive Woolly Buggers #6–10; Olive, Black, or Blood Leech #8.

When to Fish
The best fishing starts around the end of May and continues through July. The salmonfly hatch in late May or early June is one of the highlights of the season.

Seasons & Limits
This stream used to be a fly fishing, artificial lure only stream. After a test period of several years with no measurable change in the fishing quality, the regulations were changed back to an eight-fish limit. Check current Utah Fishing Proclamation.

Accommodations & Services
There are campsites along Blacksmith Fork and up its tributary, Left Hand Fork. Logan and the Cache Valley offer a variety of comfortable hotels and restaurants.

Nearby Fly Fishing
Logan River and the Left Hand Fork of the Blacksmith Fork.

Rating
Because of its general regulations and comparability to the state's best fisheries, I give the Blacksmith Fork a 7.

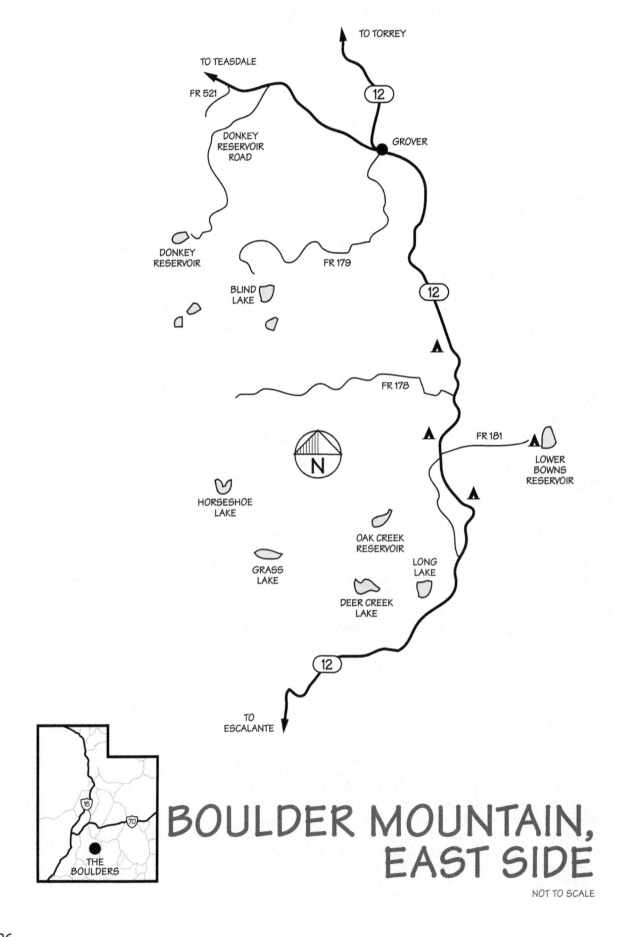

TO TORREY

TO TEASDALE

FR 521

12

DONKEY RESERVOIR ROAD

GROVER

DONKEY RESERVOIR

FR 179

BLIND LAKE

12

FR 178

N

HORSESHOE LAKE

FR 181

LOWER BOWNS RESERVOIR

OAK CREEK RESERVOIR

LONG LAKE

GRASS LAKE

DEER CREEK LAKE

12

TO ESCALANTE

15

70

THE BOULDERS

BOULDER MOUNTAIN, EAST SIDE

NOT TO SCALE

Boulder Mountain, East Side

Located approximately 200 miles southeast of Salt Lake City and 300 miles northeast of Las Vegas, Boulder Mountain (the Boulders) was until just recently among Utah's best-kept fishing secrets. The 80-some-odd fishable lakes and reservoirs, some connected by small, fast-running streams, are similar in appearance to still waters in the Uintas, but the fish are larger.

For purposes of this book, the Boulders is separated into two sections: East Side and West Side. First some general fishing tips for the entire mountain region.

If fishing any of the Boulders' lakes from a float tube, concentrate where shelves drop off suddenly. Cast to shore within inches of the bank. Big brookies cruise here looking for smaller fish that are waiting for terrestrials to drop from trees and other structure. Even the bugs are big here, so use a large pattern with a small dropper.

If you are going for trophies, fish the Boulders just before the lakes freeze over or again at ice-out when the mountain's big brookies are hungry and aggressive. At these times, fish are splashing through the moss on the shoreline, kicking out big scuds—an amazing sight. You can hook a trophy brookie in midsummer, but figure on fishing after 10 p.m. with large minnow patterns. These large fish are very predatory and prefer hunting at night.

Boulder Mountain, East Side: Hwy. 12 separates the east side of the Boulders from the red rock and sandstone desert of Capitol Reef National Park. Designated one of the top-ten scenic highways in the United States by *Car and Driver* magazine, the drive alone is worth the visit. From Hwy. 12, you can drive to Long Lake and Oak Creek Reservoir as well as hike to several other lakes. Two very rough roads provide access to the Boulders off Hwy. 12. As with all roads on this map, four-wheel drive is recommended.

Road 179: The road to Green Lake or the trailhead to Blind Lake (the largest natural lake on the mountain) where splake in excess of six pounds have been caught. There are several other lakes within short (30- to 90-minute) hikes.

Road 521: Access to Coleman and Round lakes and the trailheads to several other lakes.

Types of Fish
Brookies, rainbows, cutthroats, and sterile hybrids: splake, tiger trout, and brake (male brown–female lake).

Known Hatches
Ants, caddis, callibaetis, damsels, scuds, midges.

Equipment to Use
Rods: 4–6 weight, 7–9'.
Reels: Standard click or disc trout reel.
Lines: Weight forward or double-taper floating for evening hatches, otherwise sink tips.
Leaders & tippet: 5X to 6X, 7–9'.
Wading: Chest-high waders or lightweight hippers.

Flies to Use
Early Season: Scuds and Prince Nymphs, Woolly Buggers and other Leech patterns any time. Try sliding a bead onto the leader above the fly.
Mid–Late Season: Watch for ant hatches (big, #12 Black Ants with wings). Dry fly fishing is good in summertime. Evening callibaetis hatches late July, August. Elk Hair Caddis, Parachute Adams work well.
Late Season: Minnow and Leech patterns.

When to Fish
Midsummer to early fall. For trophy brook trout: just before the lakes freeze, at ice-out, and summer late nights.

Seasons & Limits
Check current regulations. Most Boulder Mountain lakes are closed November to end of April. There is a four-trout limit (two over 14"), plus up to four brook trout.

Accommodations & Services
Three campgrounds, suitable for tents, trailers, and campers, along a 20-mile stretch of Hwy. 12. Water and toilets but no electricity. Other accommodations in Teasdale and Torrey.

Nearby Fly Fishing
A destination in itself, but also try the Fremont River.

Rating
Beautiful scenery, great fishing, a definite 8.

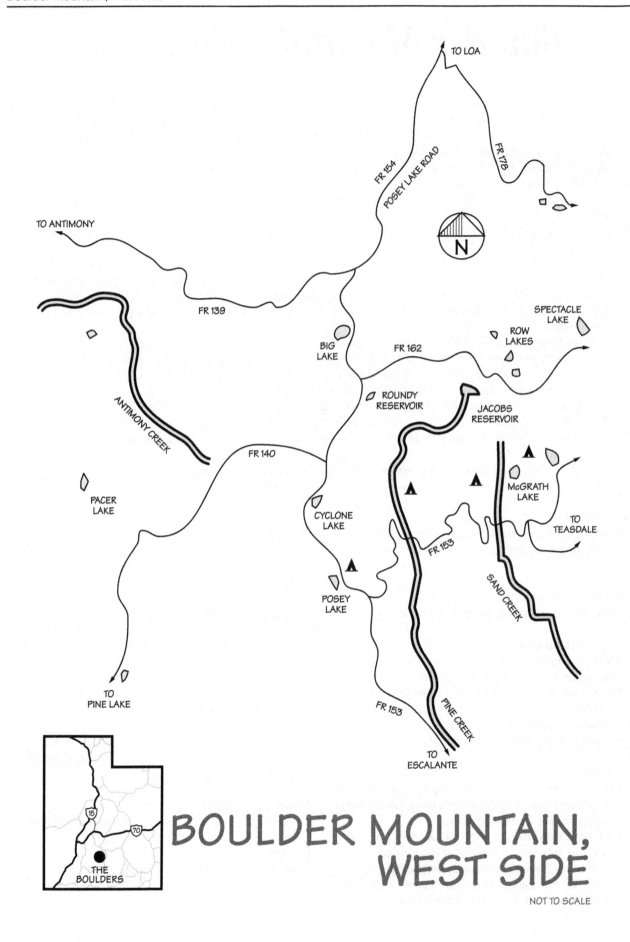

BOULDER MOUNTAIN,
WEST SIDE

NOT TO SCALE

Boulder Mountain, West Side

Capped with a 300- to 400-foot layer of lava, the Boulders are aptly named. Generally speaking, a high-clearance vehicle will suffice, but 4WD is highly recommended for all roads on the mountain. At best, the going is tough, and frequent summer showers often throw muddy and slippery into the mix. Check with the Teasdale Ranger District and station (435-425-3702) about open and closed sections of road, which changes from year to year for maintenance, habitat improvement, and so on.

The majority of the lakes on the Boulders are located on its west side with many accessible by Forest Road 154, a good gravel road south of the towns of Loa and Bicknell.

Road 178: Access to Boulder Top when open after June 15. Drive to or near Cook, Miller, Raft, East Boulder, and Crater lakes; 3½-pound-plus brookies are in these and other lakes, just a short hike away.

Road 162: Another access to Boulder Top that, going east, takes you to the Row Lakes system and on up to Spectacle Lake and the trailheads to several other beautiful lakes with fat trout.

Road 154: Goes south past Posey Lake Campground. From there you can continue to Escalante or turn east on 153 through scenic Hell's Backbone toward the town of Boulder on Hwy. 12.

The definitive map of the area is available from *Utah Outdoors* magazine (http://utahoutdoors.com/maps/boulder.htm). In addition, USFS maps are available at the Teasdale Ranger Station located at the base of the mountain.

Types of Fish
Brookies, rainbows, cutthroats, and a few hybrids: splake, tiger trout, and brake.

Known Hatches
Ants, caddis, callibaetis, damsels, scuds, midges.

Equipment to Use
Rods: 4–6 weight, 7–9'.
Reels: Standard click or disc trout reel.
Lines: Weight forward or double-taper floating for evening hatches, otherwise sink tips.
Leaders: 5X to 6X, 7–9'.
Waders: Lightweight chest-high waders or hippers.

Flies to Use
Early Season: Scuds and Prince Nymphs can be deadly. Don't be afraid to try Woolly Buggers and other Leech patterns any time. Sliding a bead onto the leader above the fly often works.
Mid–Late Season: Watch for ant hatches (big, #12 Black Ants with wings). Dry fly fishing is good throughout the summer, and evening Callibaetis hatches can be a sight to behold in late July and August. Elk Hair Caddis and Parachute Adams also work well.
Late Season: Minnow and Leech patterns.

When to Fish
Midsummer to early fall. For trophy brook trout, fish just before the lakes freeze over and again at ice-out and during the summer late at night.

Seasons & Limits
Check current regulations. Most Boulder Mountain lakes are closed November to end of April. There is a four-trout limit (two over 14"), plus up to four brook trout.

Accommodations & Services
Posey Lake Campground has 23 units, and there are three small lakes nearby.

Nearby Fly Fishing
Either side of the Boulder is a destination in itself, but while you're in the area, try the Fremont River.

Rating
A strong 8 for beauty, variety of fishing, and numbers of fish, on either side of the mountain.

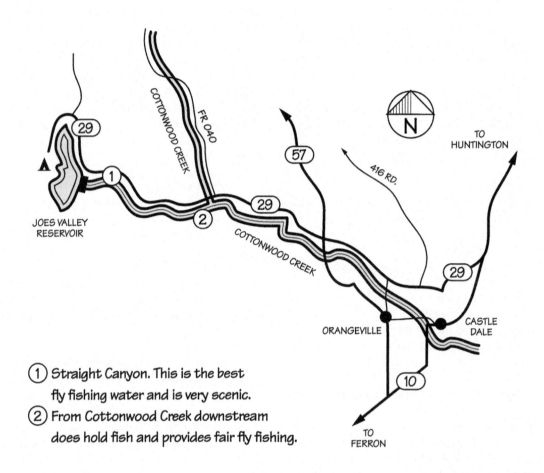

① Straight Canyon. This is the best
fly fishing water and is very scenic.
② From Cottonwood Creek downstream
does hold fish and provides fair fly fishing.

COTTONWOOD CREEK

NOT TO SCALE

Cottonwood Creek

In central Utah, at the bottom of Straight Canyon, you'll find one of Utah's most scenic waters. Cottonwood Creek flows through a valley floor of sagebrush, juniper, cottonwood, and piñon, all shaded by the canyon's towering sandstone walls.

Better still, Cottonwood Creek is one of Utah's lesser-known tailwater fisheries. Flowing east out of Joes Valley Reservoir, the creek runs narrow and straight, as the canyon's name suggests. At its narrowest, you will be able easily to reach across the water; at its widest, it may be all of 20 feet from bank to bank.

From the dam downstream there are approximately seven miles of good fly fishing water. Although challenging in a few places, access is generally quite easy, because a good paved road parallels Cottonwood Creek. Most of the year, the creek's water runs incredibly clear. However, occasional spring and summer showers will temporarily turn the stream the reddish-brown color of the surrounding landscape.

These waters flow through a veritable minefield of boulders that lend the creek its character and uniqueness. These natural obstacles, in a variety of shapes and sizes, direct and concentrate the creek's otherwise fairly shallow flow into pockets and pools unlike those in any other fishery found in Utah. House-sized boulders create deep, placid pools that hold the bulk of the creek's trout. From the cool shadows of these beautiful pools, trout will leisurely rise to take a dry fly. Nymphs also work well here, but because of water clarity and trout willing to take flies on the surface, dry fly fishing provides the most entertainment. Be prepared, however. In these ultra-clear conditions, many a fly fisher tries to set the hook too soon. Think of fishing here as an exercise in patience.

Hatches on Cottonwood Creek are relatively sparse. April's blue-winged olives provide some of the year's best fishing. In the heat of the summer, terrestrials—mostly ants—become the dominant source of food. But, no matter what the time of year, Cottonwood Creek's trout always seem to be "up" for dry flies, making this stream one of Utah's classic little dry fly waters.

Types of Fish
Stocked rainbows and wild cutthroats and browns.

Known Hatches
Blue-winged olives, midges, pale morning duns, caddisflies, little yellow sallies, ants, beetles, and grasshoppers.

Equipment to Use
Rods: 0–5 weight, 7–9'.
Reels: Standard click or disc trout reel.
Lines: Weight forward or double-taper floating.
Leaders: 4X to 6X, 9–12'.
Wading: This stream is small so waders are not necessary most of the time. On colder days, hippers or any pair of chest-high waders will be more than satisfactory.

Flies to Use
Dry Patterns: BWO Sparkle Dun; BWO Cripple #18–20; PMD Sparkle Dun; PMD Cripple #16–18; Parachute Midge #22; Yellow Humpy #14–16; Cinnamon and Black Fur Ant #18–20; Shimazaki Ant #16; Black-Foam Beetle #14.
Nymphs: Beadhead Pheasant Tail #16–20; Beadhead Hare's Ear #16–18; Beadhead Prince #14.
Streamers: Olive, Black, and Blood Marabou Leech #6–10.

When to Fish
April brings prolific hatches of blue-winged olives, which get the fish cruising the surface in deeper pools and riffles. Excellent sight fishing!

Seasons & Limits
General season, limits, and regulations. Check current regulations.

Accommodations & Services
There isn't much in the way of camping along the banks of the creek. Nearby Joes Valley Reservoir has camping facilities. The nearest town with other facilities is Huntington.

Nearby Fly Fishing
Huntington Creek and Joes Valley Reservoir and its tributaries do provide some fly fishing opportunities. Try Seely Creek.

Rating
Compared to other fisheries, a 6. For me, uniqueness bumps Cottonwood to a 7.

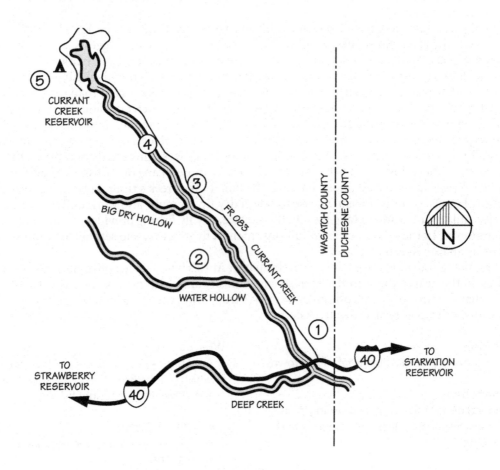

1. Less productive water.
2. Best fly fishing above Water Hollow.
3. Fish and game access point at Big Dry Hollow.
4. Series of beaver ponds found between Big Dry Hollow and dam.
5. Only maintained campground in the drainage. Facilities are minimal.

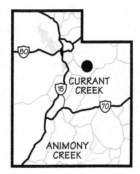

CURRANT CREEK

NOT TO SCALE

Currant Creek

Currant Creek is a small yet prolific piece of water for both insects and fish. Running 18 miles from the highway to Currant Creek Reservoir, the creek is a typical small, western freestone water that, despite its size, holds trout up to 16 inches. It's just an hour and forty-five-minute drive on U.S. 40 from Salt Lake City (past Strawberry Reservoir).

Although the surrounding countryside is not heavily vegetated, Currant Creek's banks are lined with dense willows. These willows make casting a fly somewhat problematic, but they also create areas that see little traffic. Today's shorter rods were specifically designed for this type of fishing. Given the stream's tight quarters, these rods not only offer an advantage when casting but also make life a little more interesting when you hook one of the creek's larger residents. The most productive way to fish this stream is with an upstream approach. As you might expect, long casts are not needed and will often do more harm than good.

Numerous beaver ponds are another highlight of this fishery. The majority of these ponds are located on the upper reaches of Current Creek above Water Hollow, and here you will find some of the stream's larger trout cruising and feeding selectively.

From early spring to late fall, Currant Creek's hatches are abundant. Although by no means the largest hatch, probably the most anticipated is that of the green drakes, the same large mayflies that draw anglers from all corners of the globe to Idaho's famous Henrys Fork. These green drakes are common on many of the Uinta's south slope waters, and they result in some of the season's best dry fly fishing.

Given its abundant insect life and small size, Current Creek is a great place to fish two flies. Fish a dry fly and nymph dropper that imitate the hatch of the day, and you can't help but be successful. This is an effective technique to entice larger fish, especially late in the season when the fishing gets tough.

Types of Fish
Mostly wild browns with stocked rainbows and cutthroats.

Known Hatches
Blue-winged olives, pale morning duns, green drakes, caddisflies, large golden stones, little yellow sallies, ants, beetles, and grasshoppers.

Equipment to Use
Rods: 0–5 weight, 7–9'. On this small stream with very tight quarters, smaller rods are effective.
Reels: Click or disc to match rod.
Lines: Weight forward or double-taper floating. A 5' mini-tip can come in handy for fishing streamers.
Leaders: 3X to 6X, 7–10'.
Wading: Chest or hip waders will always do the trick. During summer, wet-wading is enjoyable.

Flies to Use
Dry Patterns: Sparkle Dun; PMD Cripple; CDC Emerger; Parachute Adams; Blue-Winged Olive and Pale Morning Dun #16–18; Lawson's Green Drake and Emerging Caddis #10–12; Stimulator #6–14; Parachute Caddis, Peacock Caddis, and Spent Partridge Caddis #14–16. Dave's, Burk's, or Parachute Hopper #8–12; Shimazaki Ant #16; Parachute Ant #18–20; Foam-Backed Beetle #14.

Nymphs: WD-40 #20–22; Pheasant Tail #16–20; Mercer's Micro Beadhead #18–20; Hare's Ear #14–18; Prince #14; Green Drake Nymph #10–12; Peacock Stone, Rubber Leg Stone #6–8; Peeking Caddis #14; Chamois Caddis #14–16; Red Fox Squirrel Hair #8–14.
Streamers: Black and Olive Leech; Muddler Minnow; Light and Dark Spruce Fly; Brown and White Clouser Minnow #2–8.

When to Fish
Being a high-elevation stream, Currant Creek is best fished after runoff in June through the end of October.

Seasons & Limits
Open year-round, artificial flies and lures only, two-fish limit. Check current Utah Fishing Proclamation.

Accommodations & Services
There is a campground at Current Creek Reservoir. Nearby Strawberry Reservoir also has camping facilities.

Nearby Fly Fishing
Currant Creek Reservoir, Strawberry River, and Strawberry Reservoir are a short drive away.

Rating
Excellent number of fish and minimal pressure except on weekends. I give it an 8.

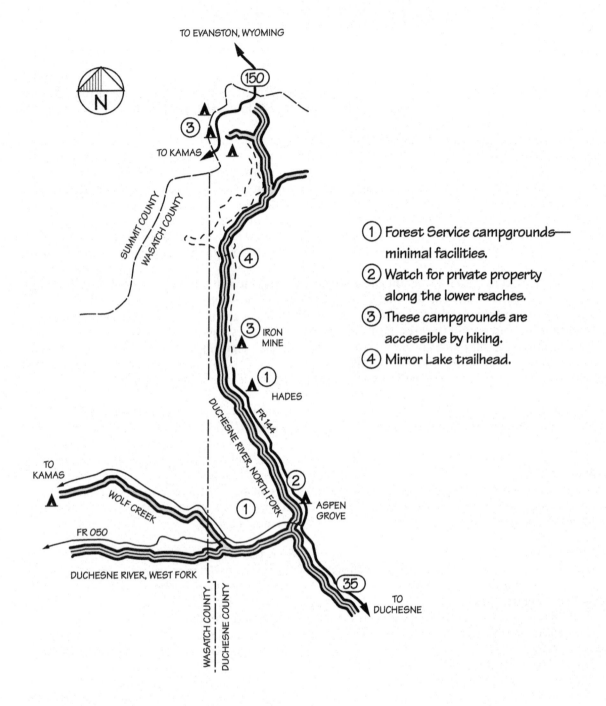

TO EVANSTON, WYOMING

150

N

TO KAMAS

SUMMIT COUNTY

WASATCH COUNTY

④

③ IRON
MINE

① HADES

FR 144

DUCHESNE RIVER, NORTH FORK

TO
KAMAS

WOLF CREEK

FR 050

② ASPEN
GROVE

①

35

TO
DUCHESNE

DUCHESNE RIVER, WEST FORK

WASATCH COUNTY

DUCHESNE COUNTY

① Forest Service campgrounds—
minimal facilities.
② Watch for private property
along the lower reaches.
③ These campgrounds are
accessible by hiking.
④ Mirror Lake trailhead.

80
15
DUCHESNE
RIVER
NORTH FORK
70

DUCHESNE RIVER, NORTH FORK

NOT TO SCALE

Duchesne River, North Fork

The cottonwood-lined banks of the Duchesne River, (pronounced 'du-shane') the largest of the Uintas' south-slope streams, contrast sharply with the area's predominant red sandstone ledges and terraces. The river's excellent hatches produce some sizable trout, making the Duchesne and its tributaries a favorite destination for area fly anglers. Unfortunately, due to the misdeeds of inconsiderate sportsmen, private property owners have closed off access to large portions of the main Duchesne over the past several years. Those areas still accessible to the public are more heavily fished, and although a stealthy angler can still be well rewarded on the main river, many more adventuresome anglers have taken to fishing the North and West Forks of the Duchesne.

The North Fork of the Duchesne is like the main river but smaller, running clear and cool along its freestone bottom. As is common in this area, summer afternoon showers occasionally wash the red clay and sandstone of the surrounding terrain into the stream, making it unfishable for a time.

The lower reaches of the North Fork are the most heavily fished, as is the case wherever access is the easiest. As you walk upstream, however, angling pressure decreases dramatically. As you move farther up the narrow canyon carved by this beautiful little stream, the rainbows and browns of the lower river are gradually replaced by a good population of brook trout. There are plenty of fish here that will eagerly respond to a well-presented dry fly, making the North Fork an ideal stream for light rod fly fishing.

Types of Fish
Rainbows, cutthroats, browns, brookies, and whitefish.

Known Hatches & Baitfish
Blue-winged olives, pale morning duns, green drakes, golden stoneflies, little yellow sallies, caddis, grasshoppers, regular and flying ants, cicadas, as well as a fair number of sculpins.

Equipment to Use
Rods: 3–5 weight 7–9'.
Reels: Standard click or disc trout reel.
Lines: Weight forward or double-taper floating lines will handle the bulk of the fishing here.
Leaders: 4X to 6X, 7–9' for dries and nymphs, 1X to 2X for streamers.
Wading: Lightweight hip or chest-high waders. Wet-wading can be comfortable in the summer months.

Flies to Use
Dry Patterns: BWO Sparkle Dun, BWO Cripple #18–20; Soft Hackle; PMD Sparkle Dun; Lawson's PMD Cripple; Rusty Spinner #16; Royal Wulff; Elk Hair Caddis; Spent Partridge Caddis; Yellow and Red Humpy; Goddard Caddis #14–16; Green Drake; Green Drake Cripple #10; Shimazaki Ant #16; Parachute Ant #18; Dave's Hopper; Parachute Hopper #6–8; Cicada #10–12.
Nymphs: Pheasant Tail #16–18; Hare's Ear #14–18; Gold Bead Z-Wing Caddis; Chamois Caddis #14–16; Diving Caddis; Peeking Caddis #14; Red Fox Squirrel Hair Nymph #8 and #14; Beadhead Peacock Stone #8; Mercer's Golden Stone #14; WD-40 #18–22. Try beadheads on any nymph.

Streamers: Olive and Natural Zonker; Woolhead Sculpin #2 (lots of sculpins in the river); Black and Olive Woolly Bugger #6–8; Spruce Fly; Olive Matuka Spruce #4–6; Muddler Minnow #2–4; Black Articulated Leech #2.

When to Fish
Starting in June, the North Fork fishes well, but the most predictable fishing is in August. At this time, most of the stream's hatches, other than caddis, have finished, and terrestrials become the main attraction.

Seasons & Limits
Open year-round with an eight-fish limit. Check current regulations for changes.

Accommodations & Services
The nearest towns are Altamont and Duchesne. Conveniently located on the North Fork is Defa's Dude Ranch.

Nearby Fly Fishing
Lake Fork River, the Upper and Middle Provo, and Strawberry River and Reservoir.

Rating
If anglers had more access to the main artery, the Duchesne would rate as one of the state's top fisheries. Due to access problems, however, I rate the North Fork a 7.

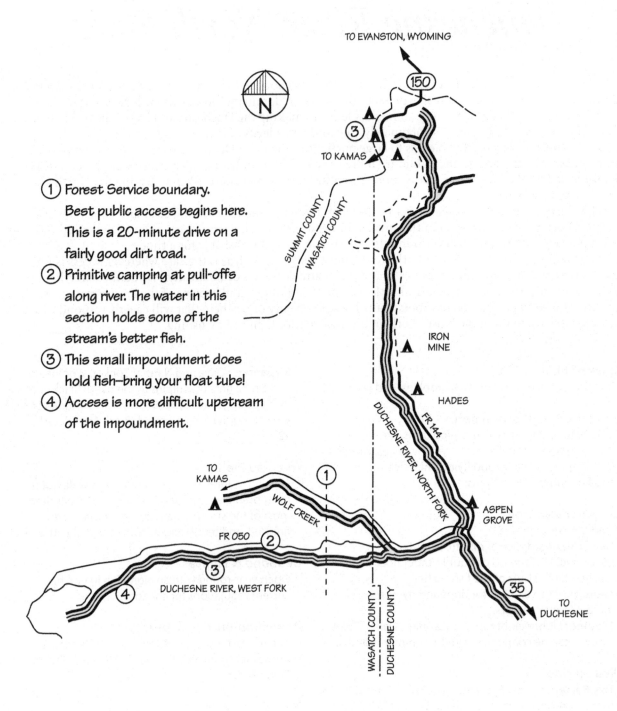

① Forest Service boundary. Best public access begins here. This is a 20-minute drive on a fairly good dirt road.

② Primitive camping at pull-offs along river. The water in this section holds some of the stream's better fish.

③ This small impoundment does hold fish—bring your float tube!

④ Access is more difficult upstream of the impoundment.

TO EVANSTON, WYOMING

150

TO KAMAS

N

SUMMIT COUNTY
WASATCH COUNTY

IRON MINE

HADES

FR 144

DUCHESNE RIVER, NORTH FORK

TO KAMAS

①

WOLF CREEK

FR 050

②

③

④

DUCHESNE RIVER, WEST FORK

ASPEN GROVE

35

TO DUCHESNE

WASATCH COUNTY
DUCHESNE COUNTY

DUCHESNE RIVER WEST FORK

DUCHESNE RIVER, WEST FORK

NOT TO SCALE

Duchesne River, West Fork

As mentioned with regard to the North Fork, over the years the main Duchesne River has been the principal focus of local fishermen. Because of accessibility issues on the main river, however, the North and West Forks of the Duchesne have become popular alternatives for anglers. Together with the main river, these two branches offer more than 80 miles of immensely diverse water. Much of it is accessible to fly fishers who don't mind taking a little hike.

Once runoff is over, typically by mid-June, the North and West Forks run clear and cool as they cascade from riffle to pool. As you move upstream on these tributaries, the prolific hatches of the main river diminish, as does the size of the fish. While they may run smaller than the fish on the main river, the trout in the upper North and West Forks are much more accommodating, as is typical of fish in most mountain streams.

To the west of the main Duchesne flows the appropriately named West Fork. Its brush-covered banks make casting a challenge. The trick here is to enter the water and work the fly in short casts while carefully wading upstream. Casts need not be long. Here, as on most other small streams, accuracy not distance is the key to success. The cutthroats and browns of the West Fork will almost always accept a well-presented fly.

Types of Fish
Rainbows, cutthroats, browns, brookies, and whitefish.

Known Hatches & Baitfish
Blue-winged olives, pale morning duns, green drakes, golden stoneflies, little yellow sallies, caddis, grasshoppers, regular and flying ants, cicadas, and sculpins.

Equipment to Use
Rods: 3–5 weight, 7–9'.
Reels: Standard click or disc trout reel.
Lines: Weight forward or double-taper floating lines will handle the bulk of the fishing. In the fall, sink tips and full sink lines work for streamer fishing on the main Duchesne.
Leaders: 4X to 6X, 7–9' for dries and nymphs; 1X to 2X for streamers.
Wading: Lightweight hip or chest-high waders. Wet-wading is fine in summer.

Flies to Use
Dry Patterns: BWO Sparkle Dun; BWO Cripple #18–20; Soft Hackle; PMD Sparkle Dun; Lawson's PMD Cripple; Rusty Spinner #16; Royal Wulff; Elk Hair Caddis #14–16; Spent Partridge Caddis; Yellow and Red Humpy #16; Goddard Caddis #14–16; Green Drake; Green Drake Cripple #10; Shimazaki Ant #16; Parachute Ant #18; Dave's Hopper; Parachute Hopper #6–8; Cicada #10–12.
Nymphs: Pheasant Tail #16–18; Hare's Ear #14–18; Gold Bead Z-Wing Caddis #14–16; Chamois Caddis; Diving Caddis; Peeking Caddis #14; Red Fox Squirrel Hair Nymph #8 and #14; Beadhead Peacock Stone #8; Mercer's Golden Stone #14; WD-40 #18–22. Try beadheads on all nymphs.

Streamers: Olive and Natural Zonker; Woolhead Sculpin #2; Black and Olive Woolly Bugger #6–8; Spruce Fly, Olive Matuka Spruce #4–6; Muddler Minnow #2–4; Black Articulated Leech #2.

When to Fish
Runoff will affect this fishery from mid-April to mid-June. July is the most productive month when stonefly and green drake hatches are at their peak.

Seasons & Limits
Closed from January 1 to mid-June. From the West Fork's confluence with the North Fork to its headwaters, flies and lures only with a two-fish limit on cutthroats. Check current regulations for changes.

Accommodations & Services
All services can be found in nearby Duchesne. There are also three private fishing facilities near the river: Defa's Dude Ranch, the LC Ranch ,and Falcons Ledge near Altamont.

Nearby Fly Fishing
Lake Fork River, the Upper and Middle Provo, and Strawberry River and Reservoir

Rating
Its remote location and size will deter some anglers, yet the Duchesne is one of Utah's better small streams. I rate it a 7.

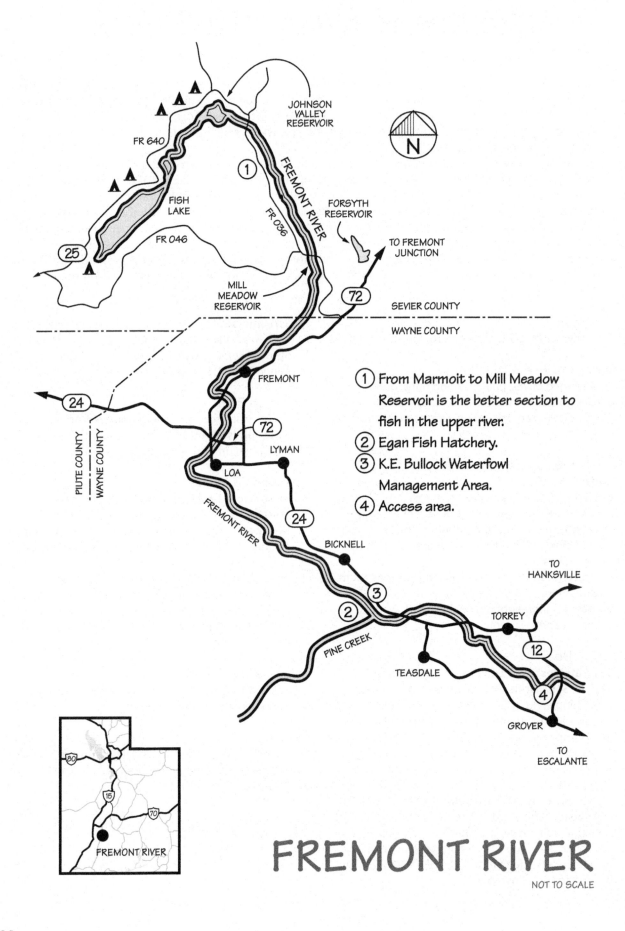

1 From Marmoit to Mill Meadow Reservoir is the better section to fish in the upper river.
2 Egan Fish Hatchery.
3 K.E. Bullock Waterfowl Management Area.
4 Access area.

FREMONT RIVER

NOT TO SCALE

Fremont River

If you like fly fishing moving water, the Fremont River provides all types of opportunities and challenges. The upper and lower sections are famous for their large, catchable browns and hearty rainbows, but this hasn't always been so.

In the fall of 1991, the Fremont was hit with whirling disease. In an effort to control the spread of this fish crippling disease, Fish and Game biologists poisoned the river with rotenone, then planted catchable and fingerling browns. This repair work was completed in the spring of 1995. Everyone expects this river to return to its former status as Utah's premier brown trout fishery. Perhaps by the time you read this guidebook it already will have! Regardless, you should definitely try the Fremont.

The upper Fremont starts below Fish Lake and Johnson Valley Reservoir and winds nine miles through open rangeland along a scenic stretch of Hwy. 25. Although less than 25 feet across, this small stream has an abundance of meandering curves, deep holes, and undercuts that provide ideal habitat for naturally reproducing brown trout. Unfortunately, because of its easy access along the roadway, this section receives a lot of fishing pressure, especially on summer weekends.

From the Bicknell Bottoms past the town of Torrey and into Capitol Reef National Park, the lower Fremont runs through a good deal of private land where access is limited. Many landowners worry that anglers might inadvertently carry whirling disease onto their property, but, on the plus side, there is very little pressure on this section and the fish thrive.

For the best dry fly fishing on the Fremont, head south of the town of Bicknell, just east of the Egan Fish Hatchery. Here the river flows through a small waterfowl management area, K.E. Bullock Waterfowl Management Area, which is open to the public. The banks along this section have been cleared, allowing unobstructed back casts, but success on this small section of open, slow moving, and very clear water requires a stealthy approach. A delicate presentation is essential if you expect to entice the wary trout that live here.

Types of Fish
Brown and stocked rainbow trout.

Known Hatches
Pale morning duns, blue-winged olives, caddis, ants, beetles, grasshoppers, scuds, and leeches.

Equipment to Use
Rods: 4–6 weight, 8½–9'.
Reels: Standard click or disc trout reels are fine.
Lines: Weight forward or double-taper floating. Use sink tip or sinking line to strip small nymphs upstream through the bank undercuts.
Leaders: 4X to 5X, 7–9'.
Wading: Depending on the water temperature, chest-high neoprenes or lightweights and felt-soled boots.

Flies to Use
Dry Patterns: Cased Caddis #14; Elk Hair Caddis; Stonefly; Dark Mayfly pattern; Chernobyl Ant; Turck's Tarantula; Hopper in July and August.
Nymphs: Pheasant Tail; Hare's Ear; Scud.
Streamers: Dark Leech pattern and Muddler Minnow for larger fish.

When to Fish
Runoff begins early here. By May these waters typically will be fishable. The best time to fish is later in the season, when the terrestrials of July and August are abundant.

Seasons & Limits
General season limits and regulations apply. Check current regulations.

Accommodations & Services
Gas, food, and supplies are available at the towns of Loa and Bicknell on Hwy. 24; there are good camping facilities near Bicknell and Torrey.

Nearby Fly Fishing
Boulder Mountain, Pine Lake, Antimony Creek.

Rating
There is excellent water here that is on its way back from whirling disease. The Fremont rates a 6 and is improving with time.

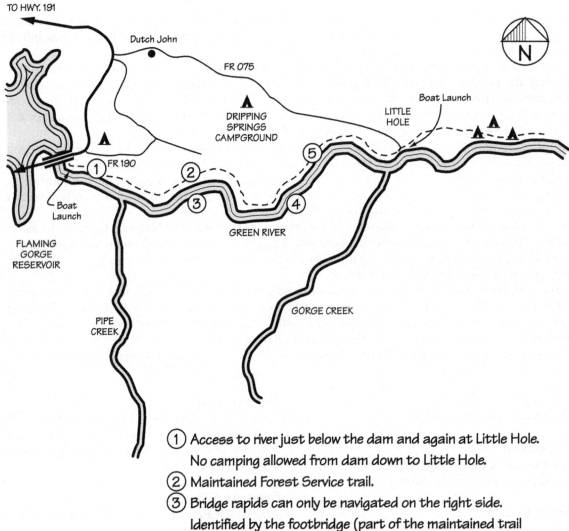

TO HWY. 191

Dutch John

FR 075

DRIPPING
SPRINGS
CAMPGROUND

LITTLE
HOLE

Boat Launch

⑤

① FR 190

②

③

④

Boat
Launch

GREEN RIVER

FLAMING
GORGE
RESERVOIR

PIPE
CREEK

GORGE CREEK

① Access to river just below the dam and again at Little Hole.
No camping allowed from dam down to Little Hole.

② Maintained Forest Service trail.

③ Bridge rapids can only be navigated on the right side.
Identified by the footbridge (part of the maintained trail
mentioned above) on the river's left side.

④ Mother-in-Law rapids is the most difficult on this section
if you are floating. Easily scount these rapids from the left
side of the river.

⑤ Restroom facilities at Dripping Springs.

GREEN
RIVER

GREEN RIVER
FLAMING GORGE RESERVOIR TO LITTLE HOLE

NOT TO SCALE

Green River

Exhilarating scenery, dazzlingly clear water, and more than enough big fish to go around make the Green River the premier trout stream in Utah and one of the finest in all the western states. This beautiful tailwater fishery was made for drift or wade fly fishing. Fish population estimates, although diminished from a high of 22,000 in the 1980s, are still an impressive 3,000 to 9,000 trout per mile, according to a 1998 study.

In 1869 the Green was first navigated by a team of explorers led by John Wesley Powell. In 1962 the Bureau of Land Management built the 502-foot-high Thin Arch Dam, forming Flaming Gorge Reservoir. which generates electricity for Utah, Wyoming, and Colorado. Regardless of your feelings about damming free-flowing rivers, one happy result for fly fishers was the creation of one of the most productive tailwater fisheries in the world.

There are three major routes to the Green River. From the north via Rock Springs, Wyoming, or Green River, Utah, take Hwy. 191. It's about 65 miles from Rock Springs to the dam. If you are coming from the west through Salt Lake City, take I-80 to the town of Fort Bridger, Wyoming, go south on Hwy. 43 to Manila, Utah, then follow Hwy. 44 to the dam. During bad weather, the most reliable route is Hwy. 40 from Salt Lake City to Vernal. From Vernal turn north on Hwy. 191, and climb 40 miles over the Uintas to the beginning of the tailwater.

The Green River is carved deep into the red rock and earth of northeastern Utah. Because of this deep gorge, access to the river by car is very limited except at four put-in or take-out points. These points define the three main sections of the Green.

Flaming Gorge Reservoir to Little Hole

Starting at the first put-in just below Flaming Gorge Dam, Section A of the Green River runs 7.5 miles through Red Canyon to the next access point at Little Hole. A USFS foot trail along the entire length of this section provides excellent wade access, but most anglers prefer to drift the river. Because of the ease of access, this is the most heavily used section of the Green.

The first four miles of the river are characterized by slow, deep runs interrupted by a few short sections of rapids. Use caution at Bridge and Roller Coaster rapids just past the 2 mile marker. In the last three miles of Section A, the river narrows in the canyon, and the resulting boulder-strewn, fast water provides excellent pocket-water fly fishing and, at times, tricky boating. Anglers drifting the river should also heed Mother-in-Law and Dead Man rapids. Both have submerged boulders that need to be carefully negotiated. At low flows, Dripping Springs rapid at mile 5 is a piece of cake, but when flows exceed 4,000 cfs, it too can be a boat-eater. Be ready!

Types of Fish
Planted rainbows, cutthroatss, and the occasional brookie. Wild brown trout and a few whitefish.

Known Hatches & Baitfish
Midges, blue-winged olives, pale morning duns, caddis, ants, hoppers, beetles, cicadas, Mormon crickets, and sculpins.

Equipment to Use
Rods: 3–8 weight, 9' or longer, depending on the size of fly and the wind.
Reels: Click or disc single action with at least 30 yards of 20# backing.
Lines: Weight forward or double-taper floating. For streamers, super-fast sink tips or full sinking lines or even 130 to 200 grain shooting heads.
Leaders: 3X to 6X.
Wading: Chest-high neoprene or breathable waders with felt-soled boots. Even though the water temperature is cool, wet-wading is common during the summer.

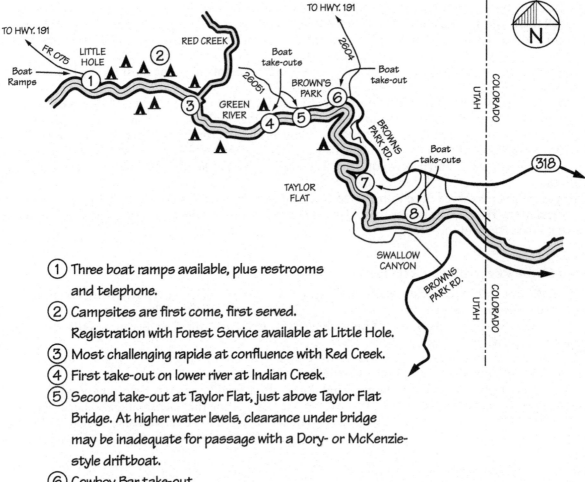

1. Three boat ramps available, plus restrooms and telephone.
2. Campsites are first come, first served. Registration with Forest Service available at Little Hole.
3. Most challenging rapids at confluence with Red Creek.
4. First take-out on lower river at Indian Creek.
5. Second take-out at Taylor Flat, just above Taylor Flat Bridge. At higher water levels, clearance under bridge may be inadequate for passage with a Dory- or McKenzie-style driftboat.
6. Cowboy Bar take-out.
7. Pipeline take-out begins at False Canyon and Swallow Canyon.
8. Swallow Canyon.

GREEN RIVER
LITTLE HOLE TO SWALLOW CANYON

NOT TO SCALE

Little Hole to Browns Park

Section B of the Green River flows nine miles from Little Hole through an area known as Browns Park. This remote valley that straddles the Utah-Colorado state line was once home to many notorious outlaws. Here, the river is not as clear as in Section A, due primarily to the silty inflow from Red Creek, which after a hard rain, can temporarily render the waters from this point downstream unfishable. There are still plenty of fish, although they are not as numerous or concentrated as in Section A.

Wade access for the first three miles below Section A is excellent; however, the wading angler must park at Little Hole and walk downriver to fish. For those floating the lower sections of the Green, access points are few and far between, necessitating long and sometimes treacherous shuttles during rainy or snowy conditions. Happily, these inconveniences leave the lower two sections far less traveled and fished.

There is one set of rapids on Section B of the Green that should be approached with caution. Red Creek rapids, approximately three miles below the put-in, is rated a Class 3. During high water flows, there are standing waves, but the Class 3 rating is mostly due to large boulders that can be quite treacherous to the inexperienced or careless boater.

Indian Crossing to Swallow Canyon

Section C of the Green begins at Indian Crossing and winds 13 miles through Swallow Canyon to the take-out point, a short distance from the Colorado border. Here the river takes on a lazier personality, with long riffles and slow meanders through open ranch country. During the late summer and early fall, there is excellent hopper fishing along the river's grass- and shrub-covered banks. This is the least traveled section of the Green, with numerous access points for anglers trying to fish this lower section by car, but be prepared. C is also the moodiest section of this wonderful fishery.

Flies to Use

Dry Patterns: Comparadun; Parachute Adams; Hare's Ear; Lawson's No Hackle; Harrop's Trico Emerger; Quigley Emerger and spinner pattern to match hatch; Elk Hair, Hemingway, Goddard, or CDC Caddis; Puffball; Griffith's Gnat; Serendipity; Double Hackled Mating Midge; and Midge Pupae patterns that float on the film. CDC, Fur, and Deer Hair Ant; Dave's, Joe's, and Parachute Hopper (Cicada or Chernobyl Ant also work very well for Hopper patterns); Royal Wulff; Double Humpy; Stimulator; Trude.

Nymphs: WD-40; RS-2; Pheasant Tail; Hare's Ear; other sparsely tied nymphs at times down to #26–28; Scuds in Olive-Gray, Dead Orange Shellback, or Clipped Dubbing; LaFontaine's Sparkle Pupa; Peeking Caddis; as well as various Pupa, Larva, and Soft Hackle patterns; Serendipity; Brassie.

Streamers: Black, Olive, Brown, or Sandy-Brown Woolly Bugger; Playboy Bunny; Black and Olive Sculpin; Natural and White, Black and Natural, Dark Brown and Natural, or Olive and White Double Bunny.

When to Fish

Fish the Green all year. The best times are in spring before runoff or dam releases and during the fall from late August through November.

Seasons & Limits

Year-round fishing. Daily and possession limit: two fish under 13" and one over 20"; artificial flies and lures only. Check current Utah Fishing Proclamation for changes.

Accommodations & Services

Red Canyon and Flaming Gorge Lodges and Spring Creek Ranch are near the dam, as are many campgrounds. Ashley National Forest and Flaming Gorge National Recreation Area cater to visitors and campers. Supplies and gas are in the towns of Dutch John, Greendale Junction, and Manila.

Nearby Fly Fishing

Flaming Gorge Reservoir, Long Park Reservoir, Sheep Creek, Browne Lake, and Carter Creek.

Rating

If a fly fishing river can rate a 10, the Green certainly does. The only detraction is that flows out of the dam are controlled by the whim of various governmental entities. This might drop the rating to 9.5.

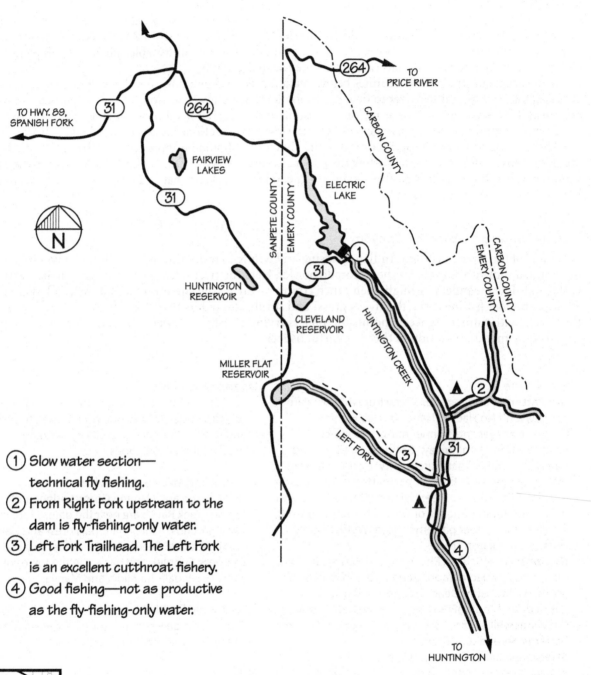

① Slow water section—
technical fly fishing.

② From Right Fork upstream to the
dam is fly-fishing-only water.

③ Left Fork Trailhead. The Left Fork
is an excellent cutthroat fishery.

④ Good fishing—not as productive
as the fly-fishing-only water.

HUNTINGTON CREEK

NOT TO SCALE

Huntington Creek

In a remote area of Utah lies a jewel of a stream, Huntington Creek. This medium-sized tailwater fishery emerges from the depths of Electric Lake and winds its way through some of the state's most scenic country. Overshadowed by a series of ridgelines exceeding 10,000 feet, this creek and its tributaries run cool, their waters rich in nutrients and aquatic life.

A short section of Huntington Creek just below the reservoir will challenge any angler's skills. Here the creek's slow, deep, and clear flow allows wary trout plenty of time to inspect your offering. Careful, low-profile wading and delicate presentations will be justly rewarded.

As Huntington Creek meanders downstream, it picks up speed and takes on the characteristics of a typical western freestone stream, running from shallow riffle to pool through a myriad of willows, sub-alpine fir, and cottonwoods. From the bridge below Electric Lake, through its narrow canyon, and down to its confluence with the Left Hand Fork, Huntington Creek has a rich riparian corridor, offering an abundance of aquatic and terrestrial insects as well as a variety of water types that serve as excellent trout habitat.

Remote enough to keep angling pressure to a minimum, Huntington Creek is a very consistent fishery throughout the year. Starting in the cold of winter, midge and blue-winged olive hatches test any angler's skill. Spring runoff can temporarily curtail fishing.

Sudden showers can often render the section of the stream below the Left Hand Fork temporarily unfishable. Once summer's heat penetrates the high country, Huntington Creek and its tributaries really shine. By mid-July, after runoff has settled and the last canyon snow has melted, anglers will find ideal water conditions and excellent hatches. A high-floating caddis pattern, especially in the faster water, is most often the fly of choice for Huntington Creek's trout.

Types of Fish
Wild cutthroats and browns, stocked rainbows.

Known Hatches
Midges, pale morning duns, blue-winged olives, caddis, little yellow sallies, ants, beetles, and grasshoppers.

Equipment to Use
Rods: 2–5 weight, 7–9'.
Reels: Standard click or disc trout reel.
Lines: Weight forward or double-taper floating for most situations. 5' sink tip for streamers.
Leaders: 4X to 6X, 7–9' for dries and nymphs, 2X for streamers.
Wading: Lightweight chest-high waders or lightweight hippers. Wet-wade in summer. Bring waders in case of an afternoon shower.

Flies to Use
Dry Patterns: Double Midge #18; Hi-Vis Griffith's Gnat #18–20; Soft Hackle Midge #16; PMD Comparadun; AK's Quill Body PMD; Rusty Spinner #16–18; Elk Hair Caddis; Goddard Caddis #14–16; Tan Lawson's Emerging Caddis; Shimazaki Ant #16; Parachute Hopper #8–10; Foam-Backed Beetle; Yellow Stimulator #14; Royal Wulff #16.

Nymphs: Brassie; Red and Brown Beadhead Serendipity #18–20; Pheasant Tail #16–20; Hare's Ear #14–18; Red Fox Squirrel Hair ; Beadhead Prince #14; Mercer's Micro Mayfly #18–20; Peeking, Drifting, or Chamois Caddis #14–16.

When to Fish
Open year-round (except Right Fork), but midsummer is best.

Seasons & Limits
From the Right Fork upstream to Electric Lake Dam, artificial flies only with a two-trout limit. Closed January through mid-June. From the Left Fork upstream to the USFS campground, including all tributaries, artificial flies and lures only. Check current Utah Fishing Proclamation.

Accommodations & Services
The nearest services are in the town of Fairview. Camping in the canyon at Old Folks Flats and farther downstream at the forks of the Huntington.

Nearby Fly Fishing
Price River, Electric Lake, and the Left Fork of Huntington Creek.

Rating
For scenic beauty, size of fish, and consistency, Huntington Creek rates an 8.

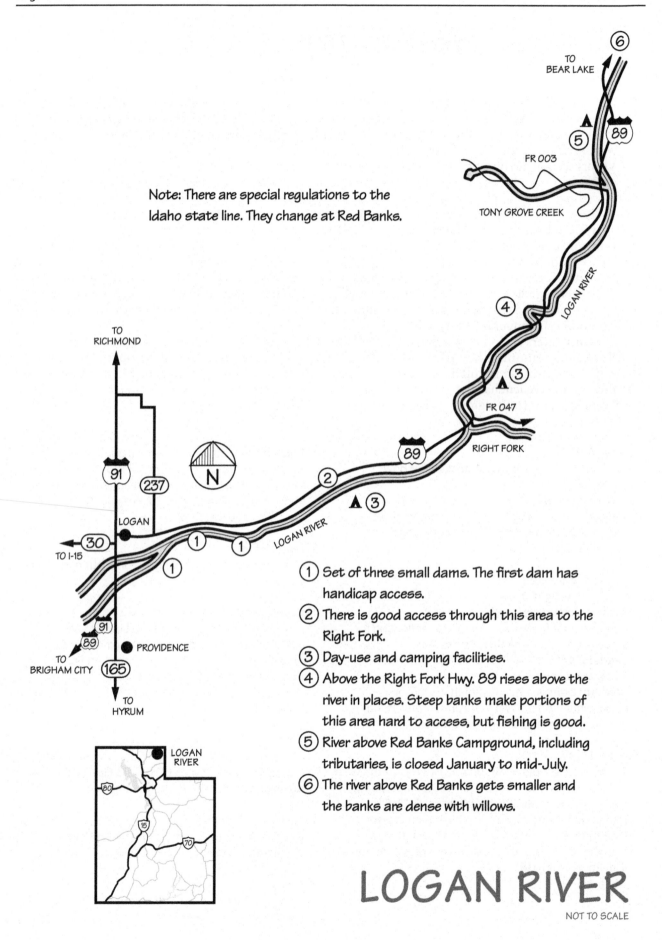

Note: There are special regulations to the Idaho state line. They change at Red Banks.

① Set of three small dams. The first dam has handicap access.

② There is good access through this area to the Right Fork.

③ Day-use and camping facilities.

④ Above the Right Fork Hwy. 89 rises above the river in places. Steep banks make portions of this area hard to access, but fishing is good.

⑤ River above Red Banks Campground, including tributaries, is closed January to mid-July.

⑥ The river above Red Banks gets smaller and the banks are dense with willows.

LOGAN RIVER

NOT TO SCALE

Logan River

With its source in the fertile valleys of southern Idaho, the Logan River runs rich with aquatic life by the time it passes into Utah. As it flows south through the Wasatch-Cache National Forest, this beautiful river passes through some of Utah's most scenic and pristine country, rarely explored except by the occasional adventurous fly rodder.

Paralleled by U.S. 89 along much of its course, this medium-sized, freestone stream offers excellent dry fly fishing and easy wading. Once the river's caddis begin to emerge, trout can be lured to a variety of surface as well as subsurface caddis imitations.

The Logan is an excellent river for children to begin fly fishing. Once runoff has subsided and the pleasant days of summer have arrived, this water is as user friendly as it gets.

The Logan's most productive water runs south from the top of Logan Canyon, where the river begins to parallel U.S. 89, down to Card Canyon. Although it is easy to drive to, here the river's steep, rugged banks present an access problem for all but the most intrepid angler. This limited access, however, also means fewer anglers. If you are willing and able, this section of the Logan is rich in wild cutthroats with the occasional brown trout thrown in just to keep you on your toes.

Below Card Canyon, access to the river improves and, as you might guess, the number of fish falls off considerably. Nevertheless, this section of the Logan offers the challenge of casting a fly to wary, selective trout. The reward is often worth the effort, because these waters also hold some of the river's larger browns and cutthroats up to 18 inches.

On the lowest section of the river, the Logan forms three small impoundments that the state stocks with rainbow trout throughout the year. In an effort to enhance the fishing, the state has imposed special regulations on the section of the river upstream of the first impoundment, and the angling pressure has been dramatically reduced.

Types of Fish
Planted rainbows (impoundments), cutthroats, and browns.

Known Hatches
Grasshoppers, blue-winged olives, caddis, pale morning duns, ants, beetles, and little yellow sallies.

Equipment to Use
Rods: 0–5 weight, 7–9'.
Reels: Standard click or disc trout reel.
Lines: Weight forward or double-taper floating lines.
Leaders: 4X to 6X, 7–9'.
Wading: Neoprene waders in the winter. Use hippers or lightweight boots, or wet-wade in the summer.

Flies to Use
Dry Patterns: Parachute Adams #16–20; Olive Parachute Hare's Ear #18–20; AK's Quill PMD #16–18; PMD Sparkle Dun #16–20; Olive, Tan, Brown Elk Hair Caddis; Olive and Tan Parachute Caddis #14–16; Olive or Yellow Stimulator #14–16; Shimazaki Black Ant #16; Parachute Hopper #8–10; Burk's Spent Hopper #6–10.
Nymphs: Beadhead Pheasant Tail #16–20; Red Fox Squirrel Hair Nymph #14; Olive Hare's Ear #14–18; Peeking Caddis; Beadhead Diving Caddis #14; Beadhead Prince; Mercer's Copper Beadhead Z-wing Caddis; Chamois Caddis #14–16.

Streamers
Light and Dark Spruce Fly #4–6; Natural or Olive Zonkers #4; Olive or Black Leech #6–8; Muddler Minnow #4–8.

When to Fish
The best hatches and fishing occur just after runoff, as late as mid-June at times. Fall is also good.

Seasons & Limits
Limit of two trout or whitefish. Upstream of Red Banks Campground is closed January to mid-June. Downstream of there is artificial lures or flies only. Regulations may change. If you plan to keep a fish, check the regulations!

Accommodations & Services
There are several USFS campsites in the canyon. Logan has excellent accommodations and restaurants.

Nearby Fly Fishing
Blacksmith Fork and Left Hand Fork of the Blacksmith.

Rating
Because of the beautiful canyon, ease of access, and wadability, the Logan rates a 7.

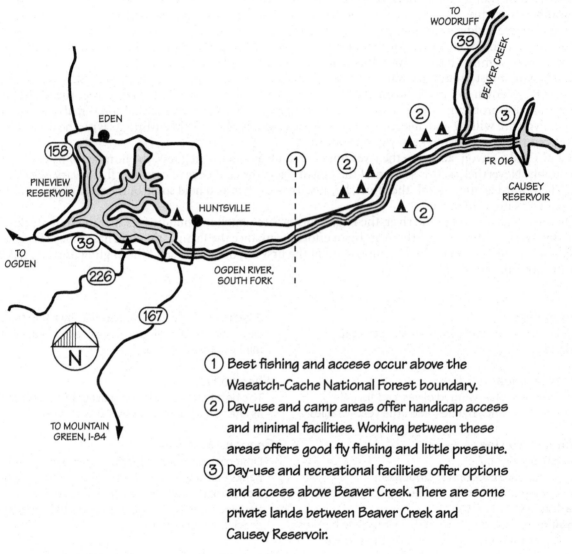

① Best fishing and access occur above the Wasatch-Cache National Forest boundary.

② Day-use and camp areas offer handicap access and minimal facilities. Working between these areas offers good fly fishing and little pressure.

③ Day-use and recreational facilities offer options and access above Beaver Creek. There are some private lands between Beaver Creek and Causey Reservoir.

OGDEN RIVER, SOUTH FORK

NOT TO SCALE

Ogden River, South Fork

The South Fork of the Ogden River flows out of Causey Reservoir through the surrounding hills with large cottonwood stands, and into Pineview Reservoir. Although not a large tailwater by western standards, the South Fork's relatively consistent flows and water temperatures produce excellent hatches and, at times, some rather large trout.

The South Fork of the Ogden is easy to get to and has several excellent access points. To fish these waters effectively and in relative solitude, work upstream from access point to access point. This water still sees little traffic. A note of caution, however: Unlike some other western states, Utah does not allow trespass below the high-water mark of rivers. Unless you have the owner's permission, passage through private property is not permitted.

Freestone in nature, the South Fork of the Odgen is one of the few streams in the state that is home to the famous salmonfly. Although present in other local waters, this insect typically emerges during peak runoff, rendering the hatch unfishable. As a tailwater, however, the South Fork is affected little by runoff, making the salmonfly hatch well worth noting. Some of the river's largest fish are hooked at this time, often on dry flies!

During the higher flows of spring and when casting large salmonfly dries and nymphs, use one of your larger rods. As the season progresses and flows decrease, the South Fork becomes a great place to try that new 3 weight rod. Through early summer, hatches of PMDs and caddis will be the most prolific. Fishing dry flies with beadhead droppers is very effective at this time of year. As the season progresses into fall, cloudy days will provide the best hatches as well as the best opportunity to catch some of the South Fork's larger trout. This wonderful tailwater is definitely worth getting to know.

Types of Fish
Brown trout, cutthroat trout, hatchery rainbow trout.

Known Hatches
Salmonflies, golden stoneflies, little yellow sallies, pale morning duns, hoppers, flying ants, and caddis.

Equipment to Use
Rods: 0–5 weight, 7–9'.
Reels: Standard click or disc trout reel.
Lines: Weight forward or double-taper floating. In the fall, a 5' mini-tip is ideal for working streamers.
Leaders: 4X to 6X, 7–9'.
Wading or Boating: Neoprene chest-high waders for warmth in the winter. Use hippers, lightweight boots, or wet wading when temperatures allow.

Flies to Use
Dry Patterns: Improved Sofa Pillow; Lawson's Salmon Fly #4; Yellow Stimulator #14; PMD Sparkle Dun; Shimazaki Ant #16; Elk Hair Caddis #14; Spent Partridge Caddis; Goddard Caddis #14–16; Parachute Adams #16; Royal Wulff #12–16; Parachute Hopper; Dave's Hopper #8.
Nymphs: Girdle Bug #2–4; Kaufman's Stone #4; Red Fox Squirrel Hair Nymph #14; Mercer's Micro Mayfly #16–18; Tan Goldbead Diving Caddis #14; Black or Natural Pheasant Tail #14; and Hare's Ear #12–16.
Streamers: Olive, Black, or Natural Zonker; Muddler Minnow; Olive Spruce Fly; Olive or Black Leech.

When to Fish
Late spring through midsummer the hatches are best and water is up a little. Good hatches of salmonflies and PMDs come off in late May or early June.

Seasons & Limits
Year-round. The limit is eight trout with only two being browns. The half-mile below Pineview Dam to the first bridge is closed; check current regulations for changes.

Accommodations & Services
Camping along the river and at both reservoirs. Restaurants and hotels in Huntsville. One noteworthy eatery is the Shooting Star, one of the best burger joints in the country.

Nearby Fly Fishing
Odgen River, Weber River, and Pineview Reservoir for crappie or tiger muskie.

Rating
This smaller tailwater rates a 6. Its ease of access from the Wasatch front range makes it an excellent option for day trips, but weekends can be crowded.

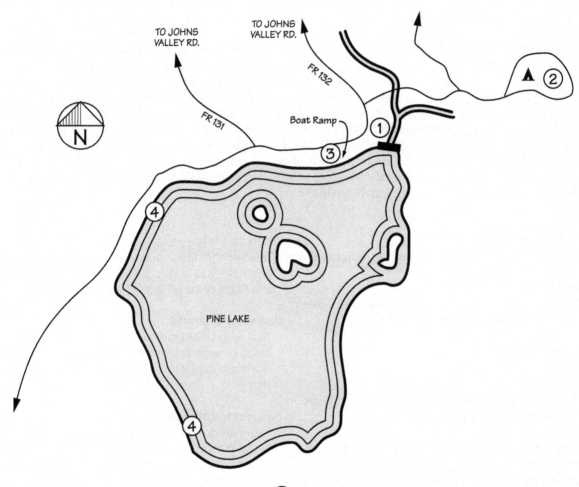

TO JOHNS VALLEY RD.

TO JOHNS VALLEY RD.

FR 132

FR 131

N

Boat Ramp

PINE LAKE

① Spillway.
② Day-use area and campground.
③ Boat ramp.
④ Good shallow/flats and structure—
best area to fish.

80

15

70

PINE LAKE

PINE LAKE

NOT TO SCALE

Pine Lake

If you fish Antimony Creek, you owe it to yourself to try another little gem in the Dixie National Forest—Pine Lake. Nestled in otherwise arid surroundings, this little still water is smaller than many of Utah's better known lakes and reservoirs, at roughly 77 surface acres. The size is one of its features that I find so appealing.

Pine Lake sits in a basin at around 7,500 feet, high enough to provide some relief from the desert heat. The lake has excellent shallows and other structure conducive to healthy insect and trout populations and is also deep enough to provide good habitat for holdover fish.

In the heat of June and July, Pine Lake is crawling with damselflies. During their emergence the lake's shallows, shoals, and weed beds are patrolled by cruising trout looking for migrating nymphs or windblown adults. Other insects are available at this time, though trout will feed almost exclusively on these prolific insects. If you're lucky enough to hit the hatch just right, you will enjoy some of the most exciting fly fishing of the season.

You can fly fish Pine Lake from shore—at first and last light this is an excellent way to stalk trout cruising the shoreline. I recommend using a float tube, canoe, or small boat for best coverage of this small lake, especially at midday. These vessels will enable you to access the lake's drop-offs, ledges, and floating weed beds where, using a sink tip or full sinking line, you will find the majority of your fish while the sun is high.

The country surrounding Pine Lake offers a variety of popular recreational activities such as hiking and mountain biking. The lake is also relatively close to Bryce Canyon, one of Utah's most spectacular national parks. Time exploring the area's incredible canyon country is time well spent.

You can reach Pine Lake by taking Hwy. 12 near Bryce Canyon National Park. At the junction with Hwy. 63, head north on Jones Valley Road. Drive past where the pavement ends until you reach FR 132, where you will take a right. Winding your way through bristlecone and ponderosa pine on FR 132, you will soon come across this little oasis of a fishery. The drive is not far, and the journey will be worth your effort.

Types of Fish
Predominantly stocked rainbows, also cutthroats and brookies.

Known Hatches
Damselflies, dragonflies, callibaetis, midges, water boatmen, leeches, and scuds.

Equipment to Use
Rods: 4–6 weight, 8–9'.
Reels: Standard click or disc trout reel.
Lines: Weight forward floating and intermediate and type-2 full sink lines.
Leaders: 4X to 7X, 7–9' for floating/intermediate lines. 3–4', 3X to 4X for full sink.
Wading: Chest-high waders for wade fishing and float tubing.

Flies to Use
Dry Patterns: Milt's Blue Damsel #10; Parachute Adams #16–20; Shimazaki Ant #16; Red Humpy #18; Callibaetis Spinner #16.
Nymphs: Olive Damselfly #10–12; Olive Scud; Beadhead Hare's Ear #16; Beadhead Prince #12–14; Glass Bead Water Boatman #14.
Streamers: Olive Mohair Leech or Woolly Bugger #10–12.

When to Fish
Best when damsels are emerging in June and July.

Seasons & Limits
Except for the inflow, which is closed to fishing, Pine Lake is open year-round. General fishing regulations apply; check current Utah Fishing Proclamation.

Accommodations & Services
USFS campgrounds. The closest city with lodging and services is Panguitch.

Nearby Fly Fishing
Antimony Creek.

Rating
Compared to other still waters in Utah, Pine Lake rates a 6, but I should bump this little reservoir higher because of the scenery.

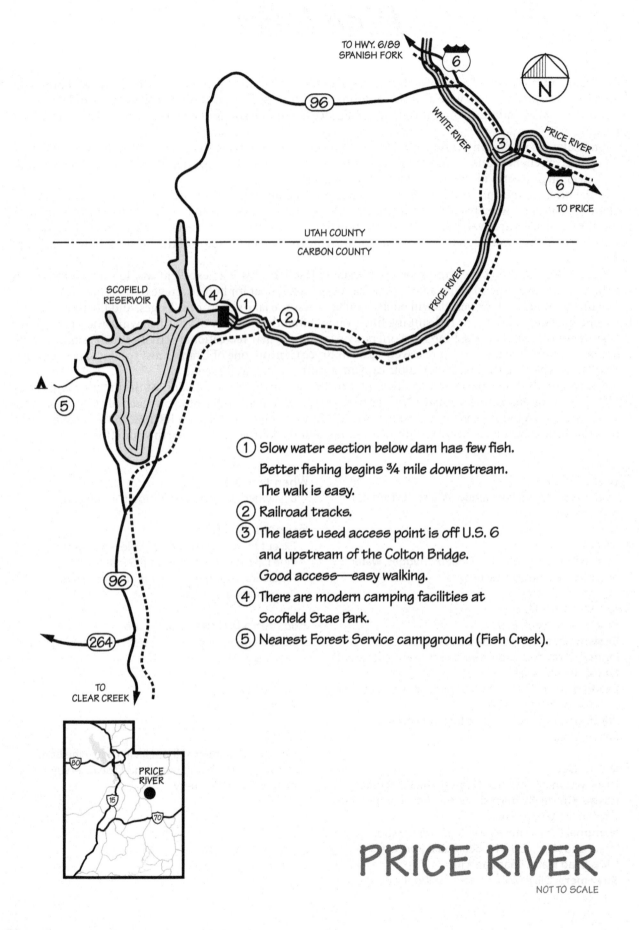

TO HWY. 6/89
SPANISH FORK

6

96

WHITE RIVER

PRICE RIVER

3

6

TO PRICE

UTAH COUNTY

CARBON COUNTY

SCOFIELD
RESERVOIR

PRICE RIVER

4

1

2

5

96

264

TO
CLEAR CREEK

① Slow water section below dam has few fish.
Better fishing begins ¾ mile downstream.
The walk is easy.

② Railroad tracks.

③ The least used access point is off U.S. 6
and upstream of the Colton Bridge.
Good access—easy walking.

④ There are modern camping facilities at
Scofield Stae Park.

⑤ Nearest Forest Service campground (Fish Creek).

80

PRICE
RIVER

15

70

PRICE RIVER

NOT TO SCALE

Price River

Although located in a remote part of the state, the Price River, spilling from the bottom of Scofield Reservoir, is another of Utah's good tailwater fisheries. Perceived fishing pressure on the upper river (below the dam) as well as muddy flows on the lower Price have kept many fly anglers away from this fine trout fishery.

From about a mile downstream of Scofield Reservoir until its confluence with the appropriately named White River, the Price is a clear-running, medium-sized freestone stream. Along this typically uncrowded, nine-mile stretch of pocket water, you will find good mayfly and excellent caddis hatches. During the optimal flows of early summer, the Price's 12- to 16-inch brown trout readily accept a well-presented caddis pattern.

During the low, clear flows of late summer and fall, the Price fishes best early and late in the day when the sun is off the water. You should also be more careful with your pattern selection and presentation. Wade carefully upstream while fishing a caddis close to overhanging willows and grasses. On bright days, a hopper pattern fished with a beadhead dropper will also entice trout out of their shadowy lies. Although hatches are minimal, fall is when this fishery is most peaceful. Most visitors have left, and trout are only occasionally tested by the few remaining anglers.

A set of seldom-used Southern Pacific Railroad tracks parallels the Price for most of its length, so hiking up- or downstream is relatively easy from access points such as the river's junction with U.S. 6. A 4WD dirt road off U.S. 6 leads to the middle sections of the river. This road's clay substrate can be as slick as ice on rainy days.

Over the years, stream flows have been kept well below the minimum needed to sustain this fishery. The Stonefly Society's recent purchase of water on the Price should help to maintain acceptable flows and restore the fishery. Aesthetically, however, the Price River is a beautiful, uncrowded trout stream, especially if you're willing to walk.

Types of Fish
Wild browns and planted rainbows and cutthroats.

Known Hatches
Midges, pale morning duns, blue-winged olives, caddis, little yellow sallies, hoppers, ants, and beetles.

Equipment to Use
Rods: 0–5 weight, 7–9'.
Reels: Standard click or disc trout reel.
Lines: Weight forward or double-taper floating.
Leaders: 4X to 6X, 7½–9' for dries and nymphs; 2X, 7½' for streamers.
Wading: Lightweight waders and felt-soled wading boots. Wet-wade in summer.

Flies to Use
Dry Patterns: Suspended Midge #20–22; Double Midge; Hi-Vis Griffith's Gnat #18; PMD Sparkle Dun; PMD Cripple #16–18; BWO Sparkle Dun #18–20; Goddard Caddis #14–16; Peacock Caddis #16; Parachute Hopper #6–8; Shimazaki Ant #16; Royal Wulff #14–16; Red or Yellow Humpy #16.
Nymphs: Pheasant Tail #16–20; Olive WD-40 #18–22; Hare's Ear #14–16; Tan Beadhead Diving Caddis #14; Brown or Olive Beadhead Serendipity #20; Chamois Caddis #14; Mercer's Micro Mayfly #18–20.

Streamers:
Olive or Black Mohair Leech #6–8; Light or Olive Spruce Fly #4; Marabou Muddler #4.

When to Fish
Best after the Fourth of July weekend. Crowds are down and the hatches are still very good.

Seasons & Limits
Open year-round. Artificial flies and lures only; limit four trout. Check current regulations for changes.

Accommodations & Services
Several modern camping facilities on Scofield Reservoir and in the state park. The Fish Creek Campground is on the west side of the reservoir. The nearest city is Price.

Nearby Fly Fishing
Huntington Creek and upper Fish Creek west of Scofield Reservoir. The rainbow fishing in the reservoir has been improving over the years.

Rating
This beautiful, uncrowded little stream with inconsistent flows rates a 6.

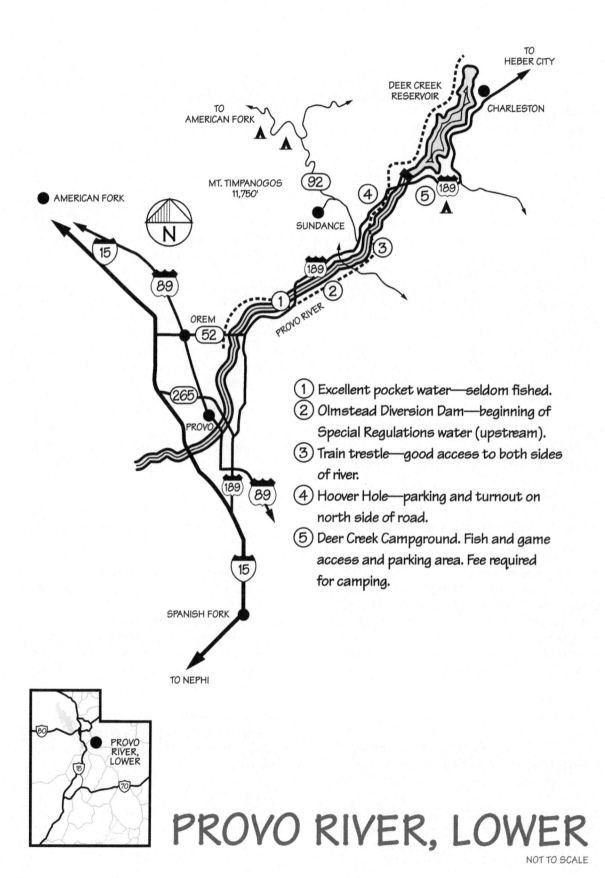

1. Excellent pocket water—seldom fished.
2. Olmstead Diversion Dam—beginning of Special Regulations water (upstream).
3. Train trestle—good access to both sides of river.
4. Hoover Hole—parking and turnout on north side of road.
5. Deer Creek Campground. Fish and game access and parking area. Fee required for camping.

PROVO RIVER, LOWER

NOT TO SCALE

Provo River, Lower

The lower Provo is Utah's best wild brown trout stream. Shadowed by spectacular Mount Timpanogas, the lower section of the Provo flows from Deer Creek Dam through the narrow confines of Provo Canyon. Considered a classic nymphing river, the Provo has prolific hatches that produce tremendous dry fly fishing as well.

Although not as easy to fish as other waters in the state, the seven-mile blue ribbon stretch of the lower Provo between Olmstead Diversion Dam and Deer Creek Dam, is still a popular destination for anglers from all over the West. Recent increases in the numbers of rainbows and cutthroats have added to the diversity of this lower section.

Because of its proximity to the major population centers along the Wasatch front range, the blue ribbon section of the lower Provo is under tremendous pressure from anglers and other outdoor enthusiasts during the warmer months from late spring to early fall. If your only opportunity to fish the river occurs during this time, you might want to consider the—dare I say it—bait fishing section between Olmstead Diversion Dam and the mouth of Provo Canyon. This section receives very little pressure compared to the upstream trophy water and still provides excellent fishing. The river is smaller, and so are the fish, but there are plenty of healthy brown trout.

Throughout the year, trout in the lower Provo feed on sow bugs. These aquatic insects occur in tremendous numbers in this river, so, if all else fails, tie on a sow bug imitation. Half of the time, it will do the trick if presented correctly.

Types of Fish
Wild browns and stocked rainbows and cutthroats.

Known Hatches
Sow bugs, pale morning duns, midges, blue-winged olives, golden stoneflies, salmonflies, little yellow sallies, caddis, and mahogany duns.

Equipment to Use
Rods: 4–6 weight, 8–9'. During low winter flows, use small rods and patterns for delicate presentation.
Reels: Any standard click or disc trout reel.
Lines: Weight forward or double-taper floating. In fall, sink tip or full sinking lines for streamers.
Leaders: 4X to 6X, 7½–6' for floating lines; 3X to 4X, 3' for sinking lines.
Wading: Neoprenes from late fall through winter, lightweight waders in summer.

Flies to Use
Dry Patterns: Salmon Fly #4–6; Golden Stone #6–8; Stimulator #14–12; Midge #18–22; BWO #18–20; PMD #16–18; Goddard Caddis #14–16; X-Caddis #14; Mahogany Dun #18; Hopper #6–10; Ant #16–20.
Nymphs: Olive Hare's Ear #16–18; Pheasant Tail #16–20; Peeking Caddis #14; WD-40 #18–22; Red, Olive, or Brown Serendipity #18–22. Beadhead versions work well also.
Streamers: Articulated Leech #4; Olive or Black Woolhead Sculpin #2; Olive Leech #6; Black, Olive, or Natural Zonker #2.

When to Fish
Year-round. To avoid crowds during the warmer months, fish early and on overcast and rainy days. There's terrific dry fly fishing during winter midge and BWO hatches.

Seasons & Limits
From Olmstead Diversion Dam up to Deer Creek Dam, artificial flies and lures only. Two browns under 15" may be kept, but all other trout must be released. From Olmstead Diversion Dam downstream, general fishing regulations and limits apply. Consult current regulations. The section in Provo west of I-15 is closed March–May.

Accommodations & Services
For accommodations with a little more scenery and ambience, try Sundance Resort, Heber City, Midway, or Park City. There is no camping on the river, but the nearby Uinta Mountains offer a variety of camping facilities.

Nearby Fly Fishing
Middle and Upper Provo, Jordanelle Reservoir, and Weber River.

Rating
Due to crowding, The Lower Provo generally rates an 8. If you pick your days, however, it can be a 10.

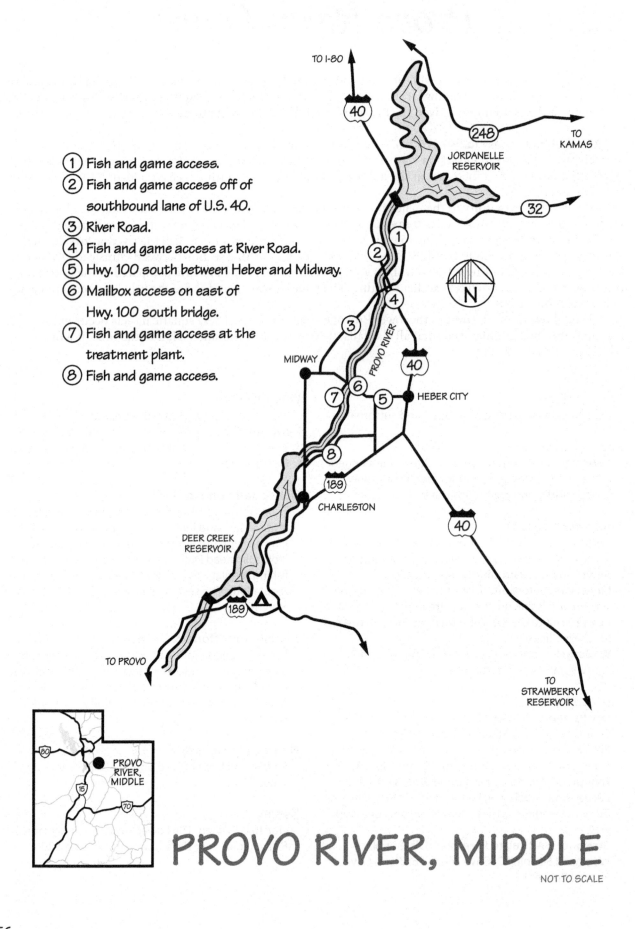

1. Fish and game access.
2. Fish and game access off of southbound lane of U.S. 40.
3. River Road.
4. Fish and game access at River Road.
5. Hwy. 100 south between Heber and Midway.
6. Mailbox access on east of Hwy. 100 south bridge.
7. Fish and game access at the treatment plant.
8. Fish and game access.

PROVO RIVER, MIDDLE

NOT TO SCALE

Provo River, Middle

The middle section of the Provo was not considered one of Utah's premier trout waters until the completion of Jordanelle Dam. Before then the river suffered from minimal flows, little insect diversity, and marginal habitat. With the dam, the Middle Provo has blossomed into one of the state's better blue ribbon waters.

Cottonwood and willow-lined banks mark the middle Provo's descent through beautiful Heber Valley. Since its transformation into a medium-sized, freestone tailwater, stream flows have improved greatly. Early in the season, the river runs high and fast. Moving water and slick, bowling-ball-sized rocks make cleated, felt-soled wading boots a necessity. By summer, the flows are much more manageable, but the stream bottom is no less slippery.

After Jordanelle Dam was completed, the most significant change on the middle Provo was the increase in the number and diversity of insects. Fishing can be good as early as March, with early midge and blue-winged olive hatches. In April, more water is released from the dam, and stoneflies start hatching around the end of the month. From this time until winter, the river is alive with aquatic insects interspersed with steady hatches of terrestrials.

Surprisingly, some of the middle Provo's larger fish can be found feeding in fast water. Do not assume that splashy rises mean smaller trout. Later in the year, casting big hoppers along the banks and under overhanging willows is a great way to spend a hot summer afternoon while waiting for the evening caddis hatch. Fall streamer fishing may produce some of the season's better trout.

The future of the middle section of the Provo River is bright. Utah has implemented an extensive mitigation plan to regain habitat lost through poor management and to acquire additional public access. Overall, the middle Provo has much to offer fly anglers.

Types of Fish
Browns and rainbows.

Known Hatches
Green drakes, pale morning duns, midges, blue-winged olives, golden stoneflies, small salmonflies, little yellow sallies, caddis, hoppers, ants, and beetles.

Equipment to Use
Rods: 4–6 weight, 8–9'.
Reels: Standard click or disc trout reel.
Lines: Weight forward or double-taper floating. A mini-tip or full sinking line works best for streamers in the fall.
Leaders: 4X to 6X, 7½–12' for floating lines; 3X to 4X, 3' for sinking.
Wading: Neoprene waders from late fall through winter, lightweights during summer. Cleated, felt-soled boots a must.

Flies to Use
Dry Patterns: Hemingway Caddis #12; Golden Stone #6–8; Stimulator #14–12; Midge #18–22; BWO #18–20; PMD #16–18; Goddard Caddis #14–16; X-Caddis #14; Mahogany Dun #18; Burk's Spent Hopper #6–10; Shimazaki Ant #12–16; Lawson's Green Drake; and Green Drake Cripple #10.
Nymphs: Peacock Stone #12–18; Olive Hare's Ear #16–18; Pheasant Tail #16–20; Peeking Caddis #14; WD-40 #18–22; Mercer's Golden Stone #12–14; Red Fox Squirrel Hair #8–14; and Prince #12–14. Beadhead versions work well also.
Streamers: Articulated Leech #4; Olive or Black Woolhead Sculpin #2; Olive Leech #6; Black, Olive, or Natural Zonker #2.

When to Fish
Year-round, but the best time is during the stonefly and green drake hatches of late June into July.

Seasons & Limits
Charleston Bridge upstream to Jordanelle Dam, artificial flies and lures only. Two brown trout less than 15", all rainbows and cutthroats and their hybrids must be released. Check current Utah Fishing Proclamation.

Accommodations & Services
Sundance Resort, Heber City, Midway, or Park City have services. Find great camping facilities north in the Uinta National Forest.

Nearby Fly Fishing
Upper and lower Provo, Jordanelle Reservoir, and Weber River.

Rating
The middle Provo is a solid 9, and if the mitigation project is ever completed, the river has the potential to be a 10. The way it's going, however, it might even get there on its own.

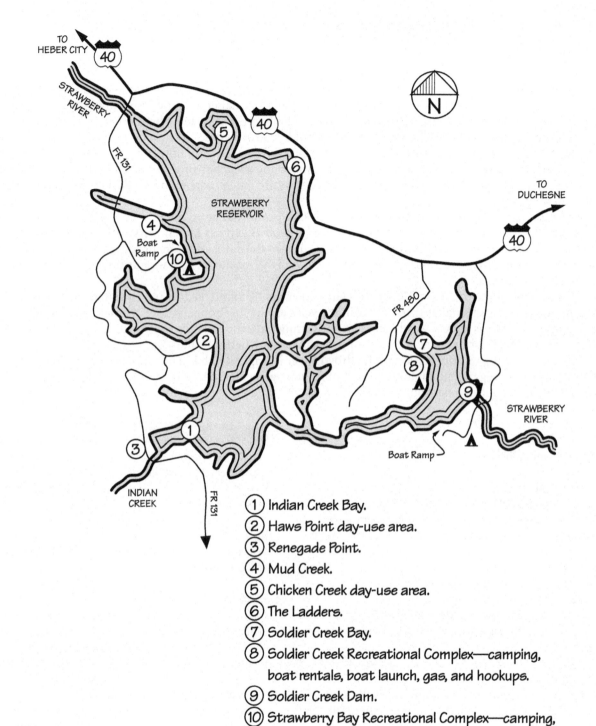

1. Indian Creek Bay.
2. Haws Point day-use area.
3. Renegade Point.
4. Mud Creek.
5. Chicken Creek day-use area.
6. The Ladders.
7. Soldier Creek Bay.
8. Soldier Creek Recreational Complex—camping, boat rentals, boat launch, gas, and hookups.
9. Soldier Creek Dam.
10. Strawberry Bay Recreational Complex—camping, boat rentals, boat launch, gas, and hookups.

STRAWBERRY RESERVOIR

NOT TO SCALE

Strawberry Reservoir

In 1980, Strawberry and Soldier Creek reservoirs were combined to create what is now known only as Strawberry Reservoir or, as locals refer to it, "the Berry." Located 23 miles east of Heber City in the meadows and aspen groves of the Uinta National Forest, the Berry offers anglers consistently productive fishing against a backdrop of some of Utah's most beautiful scenery.

In 1971, Utah's Division of Wildlife Resources (DWR) treated Strawberry Reservoir with rotenone to rid the fishery of an infestation of chubs and suckers. At the time, it was the largest rotenone treatment in the world, and afterwards, the reservoir rebounded to become one of the west's best trophy still water fisheries. The state undertook this huge project again in 1990. Once again, conditions at Strawberry Reservoir are reminiscent of the glory years of the late '70s and the '80s.

The Berry's cold, clean water and numerous shallow bays and inlets create a still water environment unlike any other in the state. Nurtured by this fertile habitat of aquatic plants and insects, the reservoir's resident trout have become famous for their numbers and tremendous rate of growth.

As you might expect from a still water of this size, the Berry offers a wide range of angling opportunities. The best fly fishing occurs from ice-out through the early part of the summer. As air and water temperatures warm, the reservoir becomes dotted with areas of dense weed beds, veritable trout nurseries teeming with life. Casting a slow-sinking damselfly pattern with a small callebaetis nymph or midge pupa dropper along the edges of these fertile "islands" can result in some of the season's best fly fishing. After a brief down time during the dog days of August and early September, fishing again picks up with cooler water temperatures brought on by early fall's clear, crisp nights. These Indian summer conditions often last well into November.

The DWR's ongoing commitment to maintain this wonderful still water resource is evidence of the quality of the Berry's habitat and its trout. Despite some past tough times, Strawberry Reservoir has long been and still is regarded as the state's premier still water fishery.

Types of Fish
Bear Lake cutthroats, rainbows, and kokanee salmon.

Known Hatches & Baitfish
Damselflies, dragonflies, leeches, midges, callibaetis, scuds, chubs, and suckers.

Equipment to Use
Rods: 5–7 weight, 9–10'.
Reels: Disc or click with a little extra room for backing.
Lines: Intermediate, Stillwater, type-2 or -3 Uniform Sink.
Leaders: 1X to 4X, 3–4', longer on intermediate lines.
Wading or Boating: Use neoprene waders due to cold water. Use a boat to cover more water.

Flies to Use
Dry Patterns: Milt's Blue Damsel #10; Callibaetis Sparkle Dun; Double Midge #18; Shimazaki Ant #16.
Nymphs: Damselfly #8–12; Beadhead Prince #10; Olive Scud #10–12; Homie Midge #16; Water Boatman #12.
Streamers: Olive or Brown Copper Sides #8–12; Olive, Black, or Blood Kaufman's Mini Leech #10; Peacock Woolly Bugger #8; White Zonker #2; Red or Black Krystal Bugger #8.

When to Fish
Ice-out through early summer. Fishing improves again in mid-September and can be very good well into November if the weather stays mild.

Seasons & Limits
From ice-out until ice-in, usually mid-May to November. Four trout or kokanee in any combination; no more than two cutthroat under 15" or one over 22"; cutthroat between 15" and 22" must be released. Check current regulations for changes.

Accommodations & Services
Camping facilities with RV hookups around the reservoir. Camping along Currant Creek and around Currant Creek Reservoir. Lodging at Daniels Summit. Heber City is the closest community with additional services.

Nearby Fly Fishing
Currant Creek Reservoir and the Strawberry River. Also the Duchesne River, the West Fork of the Duchesne River, and the Middle Provo River.

Rating
Strawberry Reservoir is Utah's best still water fishery. I give it a solid 10.

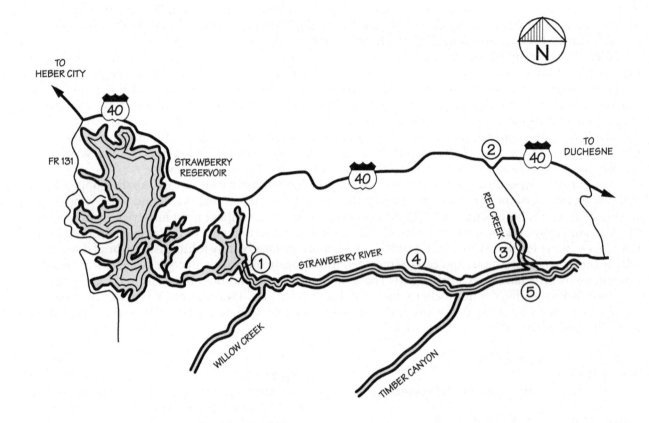

1. There is parking and easy access to the upper portion of the river just below the dam. Access here is on foot only.
2. Off U.S. 40 take the Pinnacle turnoff for access to the lower river. It is not marked well, so watch out.
3. Just beyond Camelot Resort is a fish and game access point. There are a fair number of turn-outs for parking along the river.
4. Private property here prevents access in this area.
5. Camelot Resort is private.

STRAWBERRY RIVER

NOT TO SCALE

Strawberry River

One of Utah's most aesthetically pleasing trout streams is the Strawberry River. This small and pristine tailwater fishery meanders from riffle to pool beneath the red walls and white pinnacles of a beautiful sandstone canyon. The land surrounding this unique fishery is home to black bears, cougars, and golden eagles. In some sections, this little river is as wild as the country it runs through, but don't be fooled by its size. The Strawberry River holds some very nice fish.

The river is very accessible. The upper sections are the most popular because of their proximity to Strawberry Reservoir. The first several miles down from the dam are easy going, but then scrub oak and talus make walking so difficult that only a few determined souls venture farther. For another access point that sees fewer anglers, try the Pinnacles located farther east off U.S. 40. A fairly good dirt road parallels most of this section of the river. From the road, you enter the canyon shadowed by spectacular sandstone spires, guardians of this fertile fishery.

Prepare for abundant hatches of aquatic insects as well as several types of terrestrials. If you are lucky enough to encounter the green drake hatch, you'll find some of the river's larger trout recklessly feeding on this big mayfly. Later in the season, life doesn't get much better than spending a hot afternoon wet-wading while casting a Parachute Hopper (with a little beadhead dropper) to accommodating trout. Although Hoppers are always productive, the pines and cottonwoods lining the river are loaded with ants. On windy days the Strawberry's trout will gladly accept such an offering.

Types of Fish
Browns, rainbows, cutthroats, and brookies.

Known Hatches
Green drakes, pale morning duns, caddis, blue-winged olives, ants, beetles, hoppers, scuds, and leeches.

Equipment to Use
Rods: 2–5 weight, 7–9'.
Reels: Standard click or disc trout reel.
Lines: Weight forward or double-taper floating.
Leaders: 4X to 6X, 7½–9' for dries and nymphs, 2X for streamers.
Wading: Lightweight chest or hip waders. Wet-wading can be comfortable on warm days.

Flies to Use
Dry Patterns: Lawson's Green Drake #12; PMD Sparkle Dun; PMD Cripple; Hemingway Caddis #16; Parachute Ant #18–20; Elk Hair Caddis #14–16; Royal Wulff #14–18; Peacock Caddis #14; Dave's Hopper; Parachute Hopper #8.
Nymphs: Hare's Ear #10 and #16; Chamois Caddis #14–16; Tan Beadhead Diving Caddis #14; Olive Scud; Pheasant Tail #16; Olive WD-40 #18. Beadheads on nymphs can be very effective.
Streamers: Olive and White or Brown and White Clouser Minnow #6–8; Muddler Minnow #6–10; Olive Leech #8.

When to Fish
The best fishing occurs during the green drake hatch, usually beginning at the end of June and lasting through the first few weeks of July.

Seasons & Limits
From Soldier Creek Dam downstream to Red Creek, artificial flies and lures only. Check current regulations for changes.

Accommodations & Services
No camping on the stream. Camping with RV hookups at Strawberry Reservoir, along Currant Creek, and at Currant Creek Reservoir. Daniels Summit has lodging, and Heber City has additional services.

Nearby Fly Fishing
Duchesne River, West and North Forks of the Duchesne, Strawberry Reservoir, Lake Fork, Provo River, Currant Creek.

Rating
Because of its beauty, fly fishing opportunities, and size of trout, the Strawberry River rates an 8.

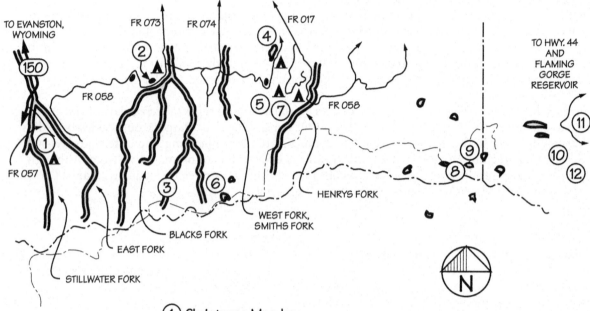

FR 073   FR 074   FR 017

TO EVANSTON, WYOMING

150

FR 058

FR 057

2

1

5   7

4

6

3

FR 058

TO HWY. 44 AND FLAMING GORGE RESERVOIR

11

9

8   10

12

HENRYS FORK

WEST FORK, SMITHS FORK

BLACKS FORK

EAST FORK

STILLWATER FORK

N

① Christmas Meadow.
② Lyman Lake.
③ Blacks Fork and its east fork are the better fisheries.
④ State Line Reservoir.
⑤ Trailhead to Red Castle.
⑥ Red Castle.
⑦ Henrys Fork trailhead.
⑧ Tamarack Lake.
⑨ Spirit Lake.
⑩ Browne lake.
⑪ Sheep Creek geological area.
⑫ Carter Creek.

UINTA MTNS. NORTH SLOPE

UINTA MOUNTAINS, NORTH SLOPE

NOT TO SCALE

Uinta Mountains, North Slope

The Uinta Mountains are divided by a ridgeline running east-west. Located in the northeastern corner of the state, the north slope of this divide is made up of glaciated valleys and meadows that are home to a seemingly endless number of excellent fly fishing waters.

During peak season, especially on weekends, the north slope sees a fair amount of pressure on its major drainages: Stillwater Fork, China Meadows, Henrys Fork, Blacks Fork, Smith Fork, and Red Castle. Spirit Lake basin, Tamarak Lake, Sheep Creek, and other waters east of the Henrys Fork drainage, although technically outside the designated wilderness boundaries, offer excellent scenery and fishing and a lot less traffic.

Although some mayfly activity can be found here, aquatic insects in general do not fare well at high altitudes. Consequently, north slope trout feed opportunistically, relying heavily on the area's abundant terrestrial populations, especially ants.

The north slope does not see as much recreational pressure as the south slope because it is farther from the population centers of the Wasatch front range. All of the area's drainages are easily accessed by road or trail during the summer. If you put a little thought into your outing and like to hike, you'll sample high-mountain fly fishing at its finest. Lucky anglers who spend some time in this endless backcountry are rewarded with unexcelled scenery and an incredible array of relatively untouched lakes and streams.

Types of Fish
Wild brookies and cutthroats, arctic grayling, whitefish, and stocked albino trout. A fair amount of natural reproduction here. The Division of Wildlife Resources stocks many of the road-accessible fisheries.

Known Hatches & Baitfish
Water boatmen, damsels, freshwater shrimp, hoppers, ants, beetles, pale morning duns, blue-winged olives, midges, caddis, callibaetis, and western March browns.

Equipment to Use
Rods: 0–6 weight, 8-9'. Smaller rods are perfect for many north slope streams.
Reels: Standard click or disc trout reel.
Lines: Weight forward or double-taper floating. Type-2 sink tip or full sink for lakes.
Leaders: 4X to 6X, 7½–12' for floating lines; 3X to 4X, 3–4' for sinking.
Wading: Depending on weather, neoprene or lightweight waders. A lightweight float tube is useful.

Flies to Use
Dry Patterns: Double Midge #18; Parachute Adams #16; Parachute Ant #18–20; Shimazaki Ant; Red or Yellow Humpy #16; Joe's Hopper #10; Dave's Hopper #8; Foam-Backed Beetle #14; Royal Wulff #14–16; Yellow or Olive Elk Hair Caddis; Red Quill #14.

Nymphs: Water Boatman; Hare's Ear #14–18; Olive Marabou Damsel #8; Beadhead Prince #12–16; Olive, Red, or Black Suspended Midge Pupa #20; Olive Timberline Emerger #16.
Streamers: Olive, Burgundy, or Black Leech #6–8; Light or Dark Spruce Fly #6.

When to Fish
Prime time is mid-July through August. September is incredibly beautiful but can also mark the beginning of harsh winter conditions.

Seasons & Limits
Most waters open year-round with an eight-fish limit. Sheep Creek Lake closed January to mid-July with a two-trout limit (one cutthroat over 22"). Sheep Creek closed August 15 to October 30. Check current regulations for changes.

Accommodations & Services
The nearest city with lodgings is Evanston, Wyoming. Tremendous camping opportunities.

Nearby Fly Fishing
All south slope waters and the Green River below Flaming Gorge and Fontanelle dams.

Rating
Due to its scenery, diversity of water, and quality fishing, the north slope rates a 10.

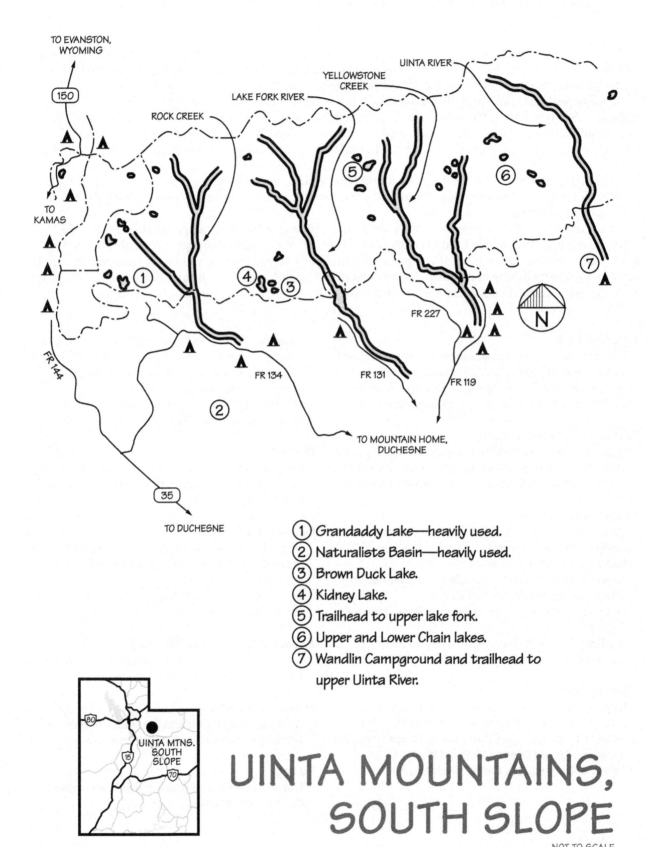

TO EVANSTON, WYOMING

150

ROCK CREEK

LAKE FORK RIVER

YELLOWSTONE CREEK

UINTA RIVER

TO KAMAS

① Grandaddy Lake—heavily used.

② Naturalists Basin—heavily used.

③ Brown Duck Lake.

④ Kidney Lake.

⑤ Trailhead to upper lake fork.

⑥ Upper and Lower Chain lakes.

⑦ Wandlin Campground and trailhead to upper Uinta River.

FR 144

FR 134

FR 131

FR 227

FR 119

TO MOUNTAIN HOME, DUCHESNE

35

TO DUCHESNE

N

UINTA MTNS. SOUTH SLOPE

80

15

70

UINTA MOUNTAINS, SOUTH SLOPE

NOT TO SCALE

Uinta Mountains, South Slope

The Uinta Mountains are home to some of Utah's finest fly fishing streams and lakes. Of the range's two slopes, the south is the more heavily fished because of its proximity to Salt Lake. Easy access and many fishable waters make the south slope a fly fisher's dream, especially if you are willing to explore.

The Provo River, Currant Creek, Rock Creek, and the Duchesne River drainages all begin in the alpine basins of the south slope, but the most heavily fished sections of these blue ribbon waters lie outside the wilderness area. Large stretches of fishable water within the designated wilderness boundaries receive little angling pressure.

Many excellent south slope still waters lie just off the beaten bath. Several areas such as Naturalists Basin and Granddaddy Lake off the Rock Creek Drainage are popular backpacking destinations. Brown Duck and Kidney lakes off the Lake Fork Drainage and Five Point and Timothy lakes off the Yellowstone Drainage see a lot of visitors. Generally the farther east you travel along this range, the fewer people you encounter.

Fishing the south slope is relatively easy because of the short feeding season and light angling pressure typical of high-elevation waters. The area's trees are full of terrestrials and, on windy days especially, trout feed eagerly on ants and beetles unlucky enough to be blown into the water. Be sure to fish the inlets and outlets of south slope still waters. On windy days, focus on the windward side of these lakes, where trout seek windblown terrestrials and aquatic insects.

Types of Fish
Cutthroats and brookies as well as grayling and golden trout in several lakes. Waters off U.S. 150 are stocked with large numbers of rainbow and a few albino trout. Splake in Moon Lake.

Known Hatches & Baitfish
Water boatmen, damsels, freshwater shrimp, hoppers, ants, beetles, midges, little yellow sallies, caddis, blue-winged olives, callibaetis, and western March browns.

Equipment to Use
Rods: 0–6 weight, 8–9'. Smaller rods are perfect for many streams.
Reels: Standard click or disc trout reel.
Lines: Weight forward or double-taper floating. Type-2 sink tip or full sink for lakes.
Leaders: 4X to 6X, 7½–12' for floating lines; 3X to 4X, 3–4' for sinking.
Wading: Depending on the time of year, use neoprene or lightweight waders. A lightweight float tube is useful.

Flies to Use
Dry Patterns: Double Midge #18; Parachute Adams #16; Parachute Ant #18–20; Shimazaki Ant; Red or Yellow Humpy #16; Joe's Hopper #10; Dave's Hopper #8; Foam-Backed Beetle #14; Royal Wulff #14–16; Yellow or Olive Elk Hair Caddis; Red Quill #14.

Nymphs: Water Boatman; Hare's Ear #14–18; Olive Marabou Damsel #8; Beadhead Prince #12–16; Olive, Red, or Black Suspended Midge Pupa #20; Olive Timberline Emerger #16.
Streamers: Olive, Burgundy, or Black Leech #6–8; Light or Dark Spruce Fly #6.

When to Fish
First week of July to September is peak season. September is beautiful but also the beginning of winter conditions.

Seasons & Limits
Most waters are open year-round with an eight-fish limit, but refer to the current Utah and Ute Indian regulations.

Accommodations & Services
Rooms in Kamas, Heber, Park City, Duchesne, and Roosevelt. Camping ranges from established campgrounds to extended wilderness experiences.

Nearby Fly Fishing
Weber River, Strawberry River and Reservoir, middle and lower Provo, and all north slope drainages.

Rating
The south slope of the Uintas rates a 10.

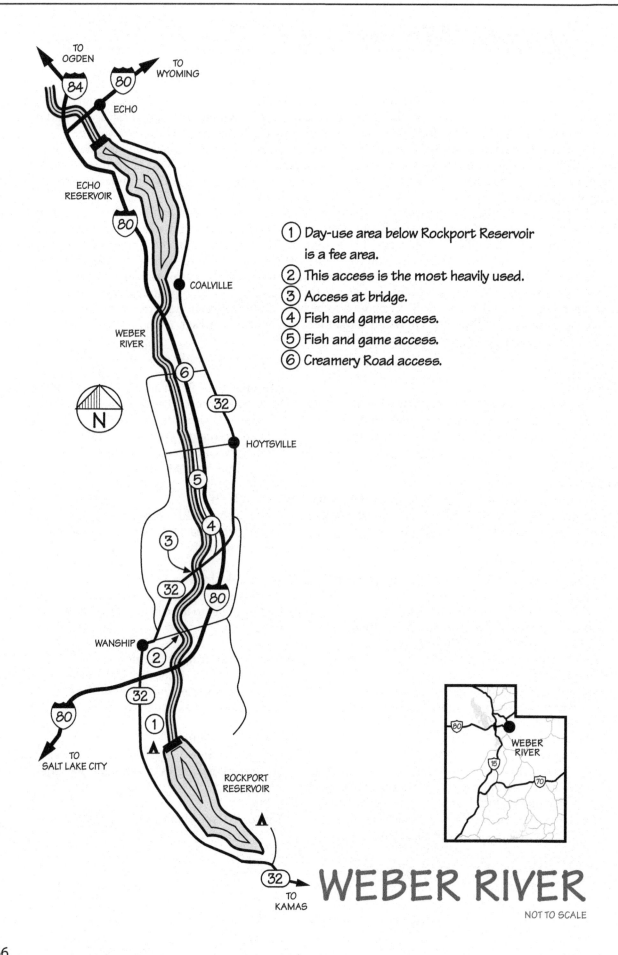

TO
OGDEN

TO
WYOMING

84

80

ECHO

ECHO
RESERVOIR

80

COALVILLE

WEBER
RIVER

6

32

N

HOYTSVILLE

5

4

3

32

80

WANSHIP

2

32

80

TO
SALT LAKE CITY

1

ROCKPORT
RESERVOIR

32

TO
KAMAS

① Day-use area below Rockport Reservoir
   is a fee area.
② This access is the most heavily used.
③ Access at bridge.
④ Fish and game access.
⑤ Fish and game access.
⑥ Creamery Road access.

WEBER
RIVER

80

15

70

WEBER RIVER

NOT TO SCALE

Weber River

High on the western slope of the Uinta Mountains, the Weber (pronounced Wee-ber) River begins as a small, gin-clear trout stream. As it descends toward the valley, it quickly takes on the characteristics of a classic western freestone fishery, which it remains for most of its fishable length. The Weber is one of the Uintas' larger streams, and its proximity to major population centers makes it a popular fly fishing destination for "after-work" anglers and others with little time.

From grayling in its upper reaches to cutthroat, rainbow, and brown trout (at lower elevations), you'll find a variety of species in the Weber. The most popular and productive sections are those with the most public access between Rockport and Echo reservoirs. As the river meanders through the surrounding valley, it takes on the flavor of a true western fishery, with cottonwood-lined banks providing excellent habitat for a healthy population of trout. Below Echo Reservoir, unpredictable water releases and turbid flows often result in a frustrating angling experience.

In the summer, the Weber has excellent caddis hatches. At first light or just before dark, a high-floating Elk Hair or Goddard Caddis worked along the edges of quiet pockets and seams can be very productive. Use short casts and concentrate on any pocket of water large enough to hold a trout. Big brown trout feed most actively at these times, and their rises can range from subtle to aggressive. Be prepared! In low-light conditions, you'll never know what you've got until you feel the trout's full weight on your rod.

During the high-water years of the 1980s, farmers dredged many sections of the river, permanently scarring its reputation as one of Utah's finest trout streams. This beautiful fishery is making a recovery, and because it is so close to Salt Lake City, Provo, etc., the Weber is still a viable getaway for urban anglers short on time.

Types of Fish
Brown trout and whitefish. Planted rainbows and cutthroats.

Known Hatches & Baitfish
Pale morning duns, blue-winged olives, green drakes, caddis, golden stones, little yellow sallies, midges, and sculpins.

Equipment to Use
Rods: 3–6 weight, 7½–9'.
Reels: Standard click or disc trout reel.
Lines: Weight forward or double-taper floating for nymphs and dries, and sink tips or full sinking lines for streamers.
Leaders: 4X to 6X, 7½–9' for dries and nymphs and 2X for streamers.
Wading: Neoprene chest-high waders for colder months and lightweight waders during the summer.

Flies to Use
Dry Patterns: BWO Sparkle Dun #18; PMD Sparkle Dun #16; Lawson's Green Drake #12; Yellow Stimulator #8 or #14; Elk Hair Caddis #12–14; X-Caddis; Olive or Tan Lawson's Emerging Caddis #14; Parachute Adams #16–20; Shimazaki Ant #16; Dave's Hopper #8–10; Hi-Vis Midge; Parachute or Suspended Midge #20–22.
Nymphs: Red Fox Squirrel Hair #8–14; Peeking Caddis; Chamois Caddis #14–16; Flashback Hare's Ear #12–20; Olive Pheasant Tail #16; Brassie #18; Ram Caddis #14. Beadheads on most of these patterns are also productive.
Streamers: Muddler Minnow #4–10; Light Spruce #4; Olive or Natural Zonker; Woolhead Sculpin #2; Woolly Bugger #6–10.

When to Fish
Good fishing from summer into late fall. In July, caddis and mayfly hatches and water conditions are usually optimal.

Seasons & Limits
Most of this section of the Weber is artificial lures and flies only, with a two-fish limit. Check current regulations for changes.

Accommodations & Services
All services in Heber City, Park City, The Canyons, or Deer Valley. Camping along the Weber's upper sections.

Nearby Fly Fishing
Provo River, South Fork of the Odgen River, and all waters on the south slope of the Uintas.

Rating
Due to access problems on the upper sections, the Weber rates a 6. With improving habitat, fishing should only get better over the years.

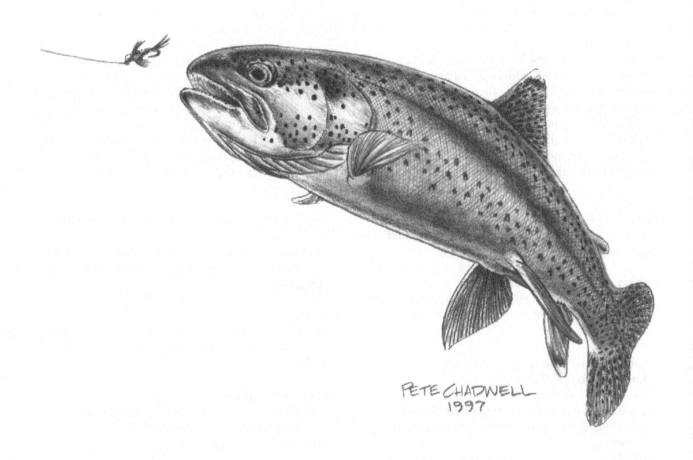

Rainbow Trout

Appendix

Utah Fly-Fishing Resources

Utah Fly Shops

Back Country Fly & Tackle
1858 Woodland Park Dr.
Layton, UT 84041
(801) 775-0489

Big Foot Fly Shop
38 N. 400 W.
Vernal, UT 84078
(435) 789-4960

Boulder Mountain Flyfishing
P.O. Box 1403
Boulder, UT 84716
(435) 335-7306
www.bouldermountainflyfishing.com

Flaming Gorge Fly Shop
1100 E. Flaming Gorge Resort
Dutch John, UT 84023
(435) 889-3773
www.flaminggorgeresort.com

High Country Flyfishers
295 S. Redwood Rd.
N. Salt Lake, UT 84054
(801) 936-9825
(877) 264-8692
www.hicountryflyfishers.com

Jans Mountain Outfitters
1600 Park Ave.
Park City, UT 84060
(435) 649-4949
(800) 745-1020
www.jansflyshop.com

Park City Fly Shop
2065 Sidewinder Dr.
Park City, UT 84060
(453) 645-8382
(800) 324-6778
www.pcflyshop.com

RoundRocks Fly Fishing
530 S. Main St.
Logan, UT 84321
(800) 992-8774
www.roundrocks.com

Trout Bum II Fly Shop &
Guide Service
4343 N. Hwy. 224
Suite 101
Park City, UT 84098
(435) 658-1166
(877) 878-2862
www.troutbum2.com

Western Rivers Flyfisher
1071 E. 900 S.
Salt Lake City, UT 84105
(801) 521-6424
www.wrflyfisher.com

Wild Country Guide Service
6531 S. Bybee Dr.
Ogden, UT 84403
(801) 791-6551
www.wildcountryoutfitters.com

Willow Creek Outfitters
9548 S. 500 W.
Sandy, UT 84070
(801) 576-1946

General Fishing Stores

Al's Sporting Goods
1617 N. Main St.
Logan, UT 84321
(435) 752-5151
(888) 752-5151
www.alssports.com

Anglers Inn
2292 S. Highland Dr.
Salt Lake City, UT 84106
(801) 466-3921

Basin Sports
511 W. Main St.
Vernal, UT 84078
(435) 789-2199
(888) 246-4867
www.basinsports.com

Fish Tech
6153 S. Highland Dr.
Salt Lake City, UT 84121
(801) 272-8808

Sportsman's Warehouse
165 W. 7200 S.
Midvale, UT 84047
(801) 567-1000
www.sportsmanswarehouse.com

Organizations

Federation of Fly Fishers
National Headquarters
(406) 222-9369
Call for local club
www.fedflyfishers.org

Trout Unlimited National Office
(800) 834-2419
www.tu.org

Lodges, Private Waters, & Services

Falcon's Ledge
P.O. Box 67
Altamont, UT 84001
(435) 454-3737
(877) 879-3737
www.falconsledge.com

Flaming Gorge Lodge
1100 E. Flaming Gorge Resort
Dutch John, UT 84023
(435) 889-3773
www.flaminggorgeresort.com

L.C. Ranch
P.O. Box 63
Altamont, UT 84001
(435) 454-3750
www.lcranch.com

Red River Ranch
P.O Box 22
Teasdale, UT 84773
(435) 425-3322
(800) 205-6343
www.redriverranch.com

Red Canyon Lodge
2450 W. Red Canyon Lodge
Dutch John, UT 84023
(435) 889-3759
www.redcanyonlodge.com

Government Organizations

National Forest Info.
1500 E. Hwy 80
Logan, UT 84321
(435) 755-3620

Natl. Weather Service
2242 W. North Temple
Salt Lake City, UT 84116
(801) 524-5133
www.wrh.noaa.gov/slc/

U.S. Fish & Wildlife
2369 Orton Circle, Ste. 50
West Valley City, UT 84119
(801) 975-3330
www.fws.gov

U.S. Forest Service Info.
324 25th St.
Ogden, UT 84401
(801) 625-5306
www.fs.fed.us/r4

Utah Divison of Wildlife Resources
1594 W. North Temple
Salt Lake City, UT 84114
(801) 538-4700
www.wildlife.utah.gov

FLY-FISHING CLUBS

Trout Unlimited Chapters

Cache Anglers 665
www.cacheanglers.org

High Country Fly Fishers 599
Park City, UT 84098
www.highcountryflyfishers.com

Stonefly Society
7012 S. 300 E.
Midvale, UT 84047
www.stoneflysociety.org

Utah Council and
Weber Basin Anglers
www.utahanglerscoalition.org

Rocky Mountain Anglers
P.O. Box 926
Midvale, UT 84047
www.rockymountainanglers.com

Clubs for Women

Real Women of Utah
Ogden, UT 84123
(435) 645-7434

Damselfly Fly Fishing Club
appleday@airswitch.net

Guide Services

John Campbell
The Outdoor Source
(702) 499-8921
www.outdoorsource.net

Four Seasons Flyfishers
44 W. 100 S.
Heber City, UT 84032
(435) 657-2010
(800) 498-5440
www.utahflyfish.com

Green River Outfitters
P.O. Box 200
Dutch John, UT 84023
(435) 885-3300
www.greenriverdrifters.com

Local Waters Flyfishing
P.O. Box 983
Midway, UT 84049
(435) 654-2235

Old Moe Guide Service
P.O. Box 308
Dutch John, UT 84023
(435) 885-3342
www.oldmoeguideservice.com

Provo River Outfitters
Provo, UT 84604
(888) 776-8824
www.utahflyfishing.com

Spinner Fall Guide Service
P.O. Box 350
Dutch John, UT 84023
(877) 811-3474
www.spinnerfall.com

Trout Creek Flies
P.O. Box 247
Dutch John, UT 84023
(435) 885-3355
www.fishutahsgreenriver.com

Western Rivers Flyfisher
1071 E. 900 S.
Salt Lake City, UT 84105
(801) 521-6424
www.wrflyfisher.com

Fly Fishing the Internet

Utah Fishing Conditions
www.wrflyfisher.com

Rainbow Trout

No Nonsense Fly-Fishing Knots

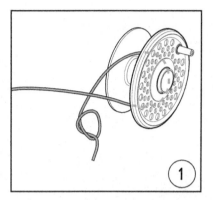 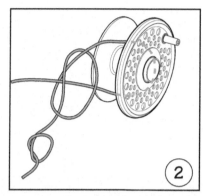 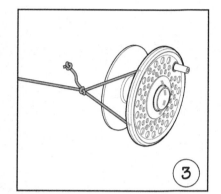

Arbor Knot: *Use this knot to attach backing to your fly reel.*

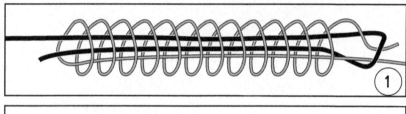

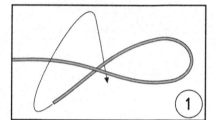

Albright Knot: *Use this knot to attach backing to your fly line.*

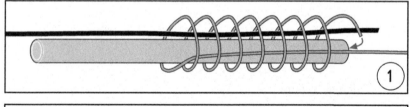

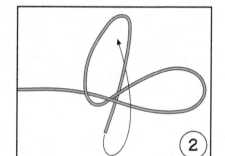

FLY LINE

LEADER

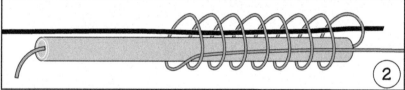

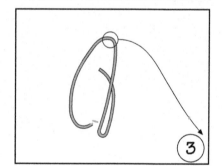

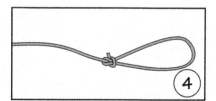

Nail Knot: *Use a nail, needle, or tube to tie this knot, which connects the forward end of the fly line to the butt end of the leader. Follow this with a Perfection Loop and you've got a permanent end loop that allows easy leader changes.*

Perfection Loop: *Use this knot to create a loop in the butt end of the leader for loop-to-loop connections.*

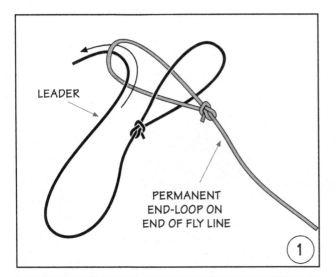

Loop-to-Loop: *Easy connection of leader to a permanent monofilament end loop added to the tip of the fly line.*

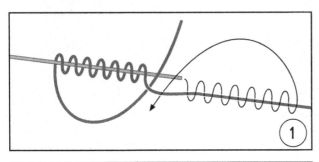

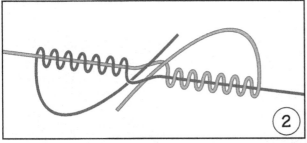

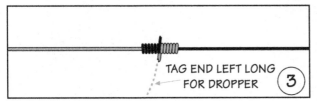

Blood Knot: *Use this knot to connect sections of leader tippet material. Hard to tie but worth the effort.*

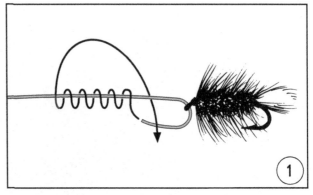

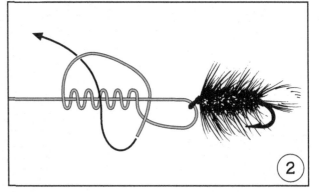

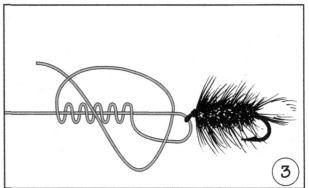

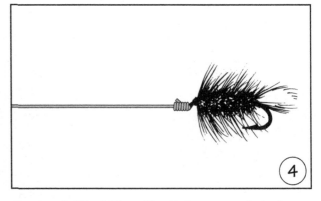

Improved Clinch Knot: *Use this knot to attach the fly to the end of the tippet. Remember to moisten the knot before pulling it tight.*

More No Nonsense Guides

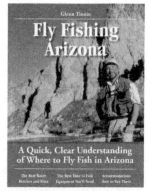

Fly Fishing Arizona
ISBN 978-1-892469-02-1
$19.95

Fly Fishing Southern Baja
ISBN 978-1-892469-00-7
$18.95

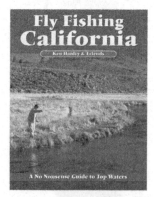

Fly Fishing California
ISBN 978-1-892469-10-6
Color • $28.95

Fly Fishing the California Delta
ISBN 978-1-892469-23-6
Color • $49.95

Fly Fishing Central California
ISBN 978-1-892469-18-2
Color • $24.95

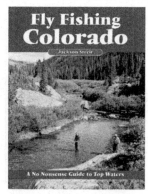

Fly Fishing Colorado
ISBN 978-1-892469-13-7
Color • $19.95

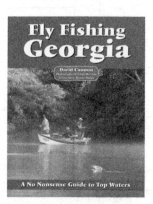

Fly Fishing Georgia
ISBN 978-1-892469-20-5
Color • $28.95

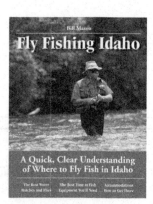

Fly Fishing Idaho
ISBN 978-1-892469-17-5
$18.95

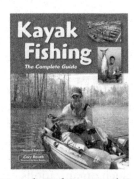

Kayak Fishing, 2nd Ed
ISBN 978-1-892469-25-0
Color • $24.95

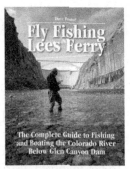

Fly Fishing Lees Ferry
ISBN 978-1-892469-15-1
$18.95

Fly Fishing Magdalena Bay
ISBN 978-1-892469-08-3
$24.95

Seasons of the Metolius
ISBN 978-1-892469-11-3
$20.95

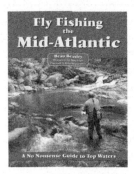

Fly Fishing the Mid-Atlantic
ISBN 978-1-892469-24-3
Color • $29.95

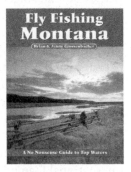

Fly Fishing Montana
ISBN 978-1-892469-14-4
Color • $28.95

Fly Fishing Nevada
ISBN 978-0-9637256-2-2
$18.95

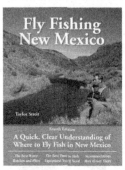

Fly Fishing New Mexico
ISBN 978-1-892469-04-5
$19.95

**Fly Fishing Central &
Southeastern Oregon**
ISBN 978-1-892469-09-0
Color • $19.95

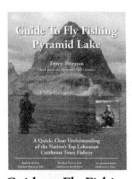

**Guide to Fly Fishing
Pyramid Lake**
ISBN 978-0-9637256-3-9
$19.95

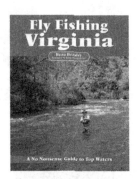

Fly Fishing Virginia
ISBN 978-1-892469-16-8
Color • $28.95

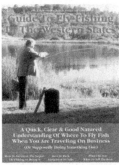

**Business Traveler's Guide To Fly
Fishing in the Western States**
ISBN 978-1-892469-01-4
$18.95

Conservation

No Nonsense Fly Fishing Guidebooks believes that, in addition to local information and gear, fly fishers need clean water and healthy fish. We encourage preservation, improvement, conservation, enjoyment, and understanding of our waters and their inhabitants. While fly fishing, take care of the place, practice catch and release, and try to avoid spawning fish.

When you aren't fly fishing, a good way to help all things wild and aquatic is to support organizations dedicated to these ideas. We encourage you to get involved, learn more, and to join such organizations.

State of Utah
Major Highway Network

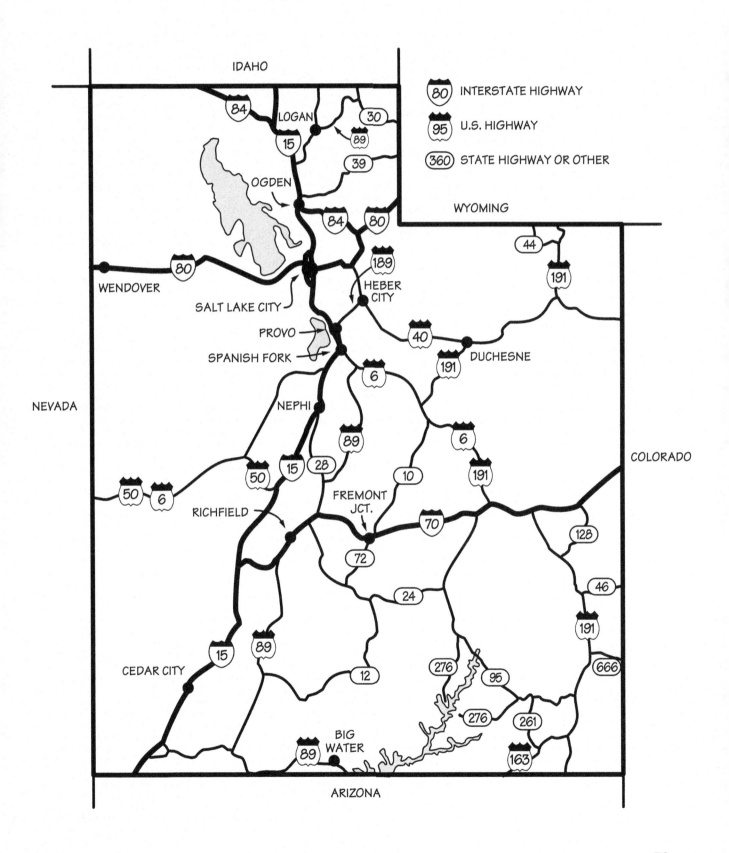

CPSIA information can be obtained
at www.ICGtesting.com
Printed in the USA
BVOW04s1228171117
500481BV00058B/1171/P